Y0-BZA-645

SAVANNAH

WHERE TO GO
AND
WHAT TO DO
WITH CHILDREN

BY
GWEN MCKEE AND KACEY RATTERREE

ILLUSTRATED BY
KACEY RATTERREE

© Copyright 1994 by Me and My Friend Publishers.

All rights reserved.

No part of this book may be reproduced without permission from Me and My Friend Publishers except by a reviewer who may quote brief passages in a review; nor may any part of this book be reproduced, stored in a retrieval system, or transmitted in any form or by any means, electronic, mechanical, photocopying, recording or other without permission from Me and My Friend Publishers.

First Printing, 1994

Library of Congress Catalog Card No.
94-79383

For Additional Copies Contact the Publisher:
Me and My Friend Publishers
Post Office Box 16208
Savannah, GA 31416

Printed in the United States of America by
Rose Printing

Design by
Daniel L. Grantham, Jr.
Graphic Communication

ISBN No. 0-9642753-0-9

To our husbands, Clay and Tom, who have over two years offered their support, patience, and encouragement, and to our children - Joe and Katie and Mary Ellen, Tom, Jr., and Billy - who visited each of these sites with us and offered their insights.

TABLE OF CONTENTS

To avoid inconvenience, readers are advised to call sites before visiting to confirm hours, days open, and admission fees.

ACKNOWLEDGEMENTS

We would like to thank the Savannah/Chatham County Area Chamber of Commerce for allowing the use of their maps in organizing this guide. We also thank the staff at each site who took the time to review our write-up for accuracy of the information presented. Finally, we would like to thank Dale Thorpe and Lew Tate for their critical review of our manuscript.

Gwen McKee

Kacey Ratterree

SAVANNAH IS SPECIAL

■ ■

Whether you are a native of Savannah, a newcomer, or a visitor, we think you will agree that Savannah is a special place. Graceful and magnificent live oaks shade the squares and streets of a city founded in 1733 as America's first planned city. Historic, geographic, and archaeologic surprises are intertwined at many of the sites included in this book. Young visitors will delight to hear tales of pirates and shang-haied sailors, to explore forts built like castles, and to wander along nature trails. Girl Scouts making their pilgrimage to Savannah to see the birthplace of Juliette Gordon Low will discover that Savannah was also home to writer Flannery O'Connor and sculptor Ulysses Davis. Wildlife, sea life, Revolutionary and Civil War history are juxtaposed in entertaining ways.

Fortunately, there are many sites to visit in and near Savannah. Opportunities for children are plentiful, providing glimpses of life in a port city which has been a bustling hub for nearly three centuries. We felt it was appropriate to have a book that introduces children to that which is unique to Savannah and Chatham County. The book is designed to be used in many ways: to help teachers plan field trips, to introduce new families to what our community offers, to assist visitors in making the most of their stay here, and to inspire adventures for any group or occasion.

Having five children under the age of thirteen between us, we continually seek ideas for weekend and summer outings. This book represents our findings. We have had a wonderful excuse to revisit our favorite places in Savannah as well as to discover new ones. Our children have enjoyed our project as they and their friends have "reviewed" the sites with us. Your children and grandchildren will enjoy these youthful comments about our adventures.

We hope you will find this book "user-friendly" and that it will encourage you and your children to discover and treasure what makes Savannah special.

DOWNTOWN/
HISTORIC DISTRICT

■ ■

1. Beach Institute African-American Cultural Arts Center
2. City Market and Art Center at City Market
3. Historic Railroad Shops
4. Juliette Gordon Low Birthplace
5. King-Tisdell Cottage
6. Massie Heritage Interpretation Center
7. Negro Heritage Trail Tour
8. The Pirates' House
9. River Street and Bay Street
10. River Street Train Museum
11. Savannah History Museum
12. Savannah National Wildlife Refuge
13. Savannah's Squares and Forsyth Park
14. Savannah Visitors Center
15. Ships of the Sea Museum
16. Telfair Museum of Art
17. Mrs. Wilkes' Boarding House

The Savannah Visitors Center (featured on page 40) is a good place to begin a Savannah visit. Much information is available here, and this is where the guided bus and trolley tours originate.

One-way streets abound in downtown Savannah. Visitors are encouraged to be alert to directional signs and traffic flow.

When looking for a specific address, it is helpful to remember that Bull Street divides the area into east and west addresses.

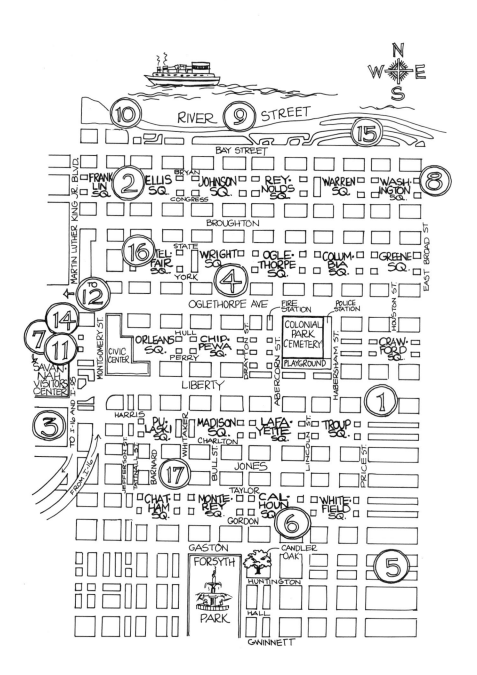

BEACH INSTITUTE AFRICAN-AMERICAN CULTURAL ARTS CENTER

502 East Harris Street
Savannah, GA 31401
(912) 234-8000

· ·

DAY/HOURS OF OPERATION
Tuesday - Saturday, 12 noon to 5 PM
Closed Sunday and Monday

ADMISSION
$3 per person

FACILITIES
Gift shop
Handicapped access
Parking
Restrooms

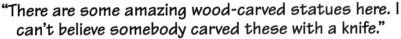

HINTS
* Allow 40 minutes
* Combine with visit to King-Tisdell Cottage nearby

"There are some amazing wood-carved statues here. I can't believe somebody carved these with a knife."
Joe Ratterree, age 9

The Beach Institute was built in 1867 to house a school for newly freed African-American children, the first such school after Reconstruction. The school was run by a missionary society and named for Alfred Beach, the founder of *Scientific American* whose generosity allowed the purchase of land on which the school was built. Several years ago the Savannah College of Art and Design purchased the building and donated it to the King-Tisdell Cottage Foundation. Today, the building features changing exhibits in the main floor galleries, an 1890 classroom, and the Ulysses Davis Collection in the second floor gallery.

A guide directs visitors through the galleries, pointing out special exhibits on the main floor. The 1890 classroom is especially entertaining for children who always seem to be amazed by the strict classroom protocol of earlier times.

The Ulysses Davis Collection, a significant collection of over 230 wood carvings, is housed upstairs in its own gallery. Ulysses Davis (1913 - 1990) was a barber who whittled between patrons and in his spare time. His work is recognized nationally for its contribution to American folk art. Using a pocket knife, Davis carved intricacies that seem to defy the scope of the tool. To many of his pieces he applied tiny ornaments for texture and dimension. A few of his works are painted. Some of his carvings are decidedly religious, others political. The series of American Presidents is particularly impressive. The collection has been exhibited in the galleries and museums of major American cities. It is Savannah's good fortune that the King-Tisdell Cottage Foundation was able to purchase this collection and make the Beach Institute its permanent home.

RUTHERFORD
B. HAYES.
1877 — 1881.
(19) PRESIDENT.

CITY MARKET AND ART CENTER AT CITY MARKET

Jefferson Street at West St. Julian Street
232 West St. Julian St.
Savannah, GA 31401
(912) 232-4903
(912) 234-2327 (Art Center)

DAYS/HOURS OF OPERATION
7 days per week, hours vary according to various shops, galleries
  and restaurants

ADMISSION
Free

FACILITIES
Handicapped access
Pay phone
Restrooms

HINTS
* Plan a visit around mealtime
* Carriage tours begin here
* Allow 30 to 45 minutes for browsing;
  more time for eating or a carriage tour
* Call ahead about special events

"I like to pat the horses."
Katie Ratterree, age 5

"There are some neat stores here where I like to buy things."
Joe Ratterree, age 9

The City Market is a two block area of shops, restaurants, cafés, studios, and galleries located in restored 19th century buildings surrounding a pedestrian-only section of St. Julian Street. It is nestled between Ellis Square, which was the original city market where vendors and farmers sold their wares, and Franklin Square, which was once the site of the city water tank. During the 1980's, this two block, four building area was renovated for specialty retail shops and restaurants. More recently, an art center, galleries, artists' working studios, and the visual and performing arts program of the City of Savannah have also located here. Brightly-striped awnings and unique signs identify the various shops and restaurants, and outdoor seating and a covered gazebo in St. Julian Street are inviting places to take a break. City Market is the origination point for the carriage tours, and the horses and buggies are always intriguing for younger children.

Inside the buildings, care was taken during renovation to leave intact much of the original structures and materials. Wide-plank wooden floors and exposed brick walls are two features that recall earlier times. The upper stories of two of the buildings are filled with artists' studios. Sculpture, printmaking, textile design, and painting are examples of the work in progress that might be glimpsed here. The Savannah Art Association has its gallery here, and there is an ongoing program of exhibits at the Art Center Gallery.

A visit to City Market feels complete when centered around a meal. City Market is one of the few places in town where there is outdoor seating for dining. Dining experiences vary from a lively pizza parlor to a casual café atmosphere to more formal dining.

City Market is the site of several community-wide cultural events. These include Herb Day celebrations in spring and fall, Savannah Folk Music Society concert (September), Jazz Festival events (September), Kid's Day Arts and Crafts Festival (October), Christmas Open House with special Saturday afternoon Christmas for Kids, Arts on the River Weekend (May), and more.

HISTORIC RAILROAD SHOPS

Managed by The Coastal Heritage Society
601 West Harris Street
Savannah, GA 31401
(912) 651-6823

DAYS/HOURS OF OPERATION
Monday - Saturday, 10 AM to 4 PM
Sunday, Noon to 4 PM
1 PM, guided tour each day
Self-guided tours all day

ADMISSION
$2.50 per person, $2 students and military

FACILITIES
Gift Shop
Food/Drink machine
Handicapped access
Museum
Parking
Picnic area
Restrooms

HINTS
* Allow an hour
* Parties welcome. Special tours can include operation of turntable and model train. Special programs such as hobo bonfire with railroad songs or Revolutionary Colorguard. Call for information.

"My favorite thing was the turntable and what was interesting was the machines we got to see."
Billy McKee, age 5

"It's amazing to see how they could operate the large turntable and the trains such a long time ago."
Mary Ellen McKee, age 13

The antebellum Roundhouse Complex and Historic Railroad Shops, a National Historic Landmark, are a fascinating step into the golden era of trains and the flowering of the industrial revolution in Savannah. This five acre site, owned by the City of Savannah and opened to the public in 1991, hosts eleven buildings constructed in 1855 and 1926 for the servicing of trains and their engines. In fact, this site contains the oldest and most complete railroad repair shops in the United States.

For train enthusiasts and others this site is a real treat, for there is a restored, operating turntable at the site, one of the few operating turntables in the United States. The electric turntable, located in the center of the site, allowed locomotives to enter or exit a maintenance stall in the Roundhouse. It is an ingenious device, replacing the original which was turned by hand in the mid-1800's. It serviced approximately 36 tracks to facilitate the repair and maintenance of locomotives. The turntable is operated for visitors upon request.

Also located at the Roundhouse Complex is a series of buildings which served as the "overhaul" or back shop, the carpentry shop, the blacksmith shop, the machine shop, the storehouse, and the tender shop. Visitors will see a 1914 steam locomotive, antique machinery, the oldest portable steam engine in the country, and an old locomotive bell.

There is an impressive 125-foot tall brick smokestack built in 1853 to draw smoke from the nearby Blacksmith Shop and the Boiler/Engine Shop through underground ducts. The museum, which is air-conditioned, houses exhibits of tools from various shops utilized in maintaining and repairing locomotives. There is also an engine display, tools used for laying track, and an old telegraph machine.

This unusual site, originally built and operated by the Central of Georgia Railway, at one time operated as one of the South's premier repair facilities. Chartered in 1833 as the Central Railroad and Canal Company, it was formed to prevent the diversion of the cotton shipping trade to Charleston.

A caboose houses the office, a boxcar contains a gift shop full of educational items relating to railroading and Georgia history, and a Pullman car has been converted to a theater which shows a 12-minute orientation film on Savannah and the history of Georgia. An additional 20-minute film entitled "Gandy Dancers" is shown on request.

JULIETTE GORDON LOW BIRTHPLACE

Owned and Operated by the Girl Scouts of the USA
142 Bull Street
Savannah, GA 31401
(912) 233-4501

■ ■

DAYS/HOURS OF OPERATION
Monday, Tuesday, Thursday, Friday, Saturday, 10 AM to 4 PM
Sunday, 12:30 to 4:30
Closed Wednesdays and some Major Holidays, including
  St. Patrick's Day

ADMISSION
$5 per adult, $4 per child (6 to 18); children under 6 free
Additional discounts for Girl Scouts and other groups;
  please inquire
Prices subject to change

FACILITIES
Drink machine
Guidebooks for sight- and hearing-impaired
Handicapped access (partial)
Museum Shop
Parking (Limited to 6 1-hour on-street places; must obtain
  parking pass inside)
Restrooms

HINTS
* Save time for a visit to the museum shop
* Special programs are available for some groups
* Groups of 10 or more are encouraged to make
  advance reservations

> "You could tell our guide liked to show children through
> this house. He was so funny."
> *Joe Ratterree, age 8*

Juliette Gordon Low may be known best as the founder of the Girl Scouts, but a tour of her birth place will surprise visitors with many of her other talents as well. Juliette, known as Daisy, was born in 1860 and grew up in this house with three sisters and two brothers. A 45-minute guided tour provides an entertaining glimpse of Gordon family life.

The house was completed in 1821 for then-Mayor of Savannah, James Moore Wayne, who sold the house 10 years later to his niece Sarah and her husband, William Washington Gordon. It originally had two stories over a basement floor. The third floor was added in 1886 to accommodate a large family. Also in 1886, damage from an earthquake necessitated major interior changes to the house, and the interpretation of the house today is based on the 1886 period.

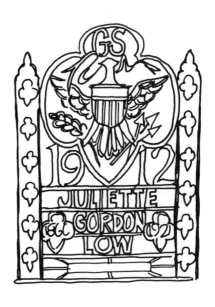

There are many furnishings that were Gordon pieces and a surprising number of art works created by Daisy herself. The library contains some of her sculptures as well as a carved piece of furniture. She was a painter also, on canvas and on porcelain, and several of these works are displayed in the house. One of her paintings is a copy of a portrait of Nellie Kinzie Gordon. Daisy had an eye for art, and the paintings in the entry hall were known to be her favorites.

The rooms of the house are large and feature elaborate decorative details. Intricately carved crown moldings and massive crystal chandeliers bespeak an age of elegance. Portraits of family members and others help tell the story of the Gordon family and the period in which they lived. Upstairs, the bedrooms are furnished with family pieces, and one room contains furniture that belonged to Juliette Low. On display are two dollhouses, sure to delight the younger set. One of these is a rare Georgia Plains style farmhouse, intact with its hinged

. front-piece. Visitors will learn about the research for the wall colors and about the use of wallpapers in houses of this period.

The garden on the side of the house is particularly appealing in the spring when many plants and shrubs are in bloom. From the garden, visitors can obtain a good view of the piazza which was added in 1886 when other major renovations were underway.

Juliette Gordon Low founded the Girl Scouts in 1912. Her birthplace was purchased and restored by the Girl Scouts of the USA in 1953. It was designated a National Historic Landmark in 1965. Each year thousands of Girl Scouts from all over America visit the birthplace of their founder and learn about the legacy of the Gordon family.

ACROSS

1. In 1886 a ____ floor was added to Juliette's house.
3. Juliette was a talented ____.
4. Juliette's last name after she married.
5. Important 1886 event for the Gordon family
9. Organization founded in 1912 by Juliette.
10. One of the streets bordering this house
11. This house and its history are part of Savannah's ____.

DOWN

1. This house has ____ stories over a basement.
2. Juliette's initials
6. Juliette may have played with a ____ like those upstairs

7. Juliette's nickname
8. An earth____ caused much damage to this house
9. Juliette's maiden name.

answer on page 106

18

KING-TISDELL COTTAGE

514 East Huntington Street
Savannah, GA 31401
(912) 234-8000

■■

DAYS/HOURS OF OPERATION
Tuesday - Friday, 1 to 4:30 PM
Saturday, 1 PM to 4 PM
Closed Sunday and Monday

ADMISSION
$2.50 per person

FACILITIES
Gift shop
Parking
Restrooms

HINTS
* Allow 30 minutes
* Combine with visit to Beach Institute nearby

"I liked the old-timey wind-up music machine."
Joe Ratterree, age 9

"I wish I could live in this house."
Katie Ratterree, age 4

The King-Tisdell Cottage is a museum of regional African-American history and culture. This charming Victorian house was built in 1896 as rental property and was restored meticulously in the 1980's prior to opening as a museum. Arriving at the house, visitors are drawn to the intricate ornamentation, or "gingerbread," that decorates the exterior. The gingerbread found here is unusually detailed for a house of this modest size. For children, the cottage seems to have been plucked right out of a storybook!

A 20 to 30 minute guided tour begins on the front porch. The interior of the house features a living room furnished as it would have been by its early residents. The house was built for Mr. W. W. Aimar, who sold it to Mr. and Mrs. Eugene King in 1910. Following Mr. King's death, Mrs. King married Mr. Robert Tisdell, hence the name of the cottage. Another room features an exhibit of art objects and historical documents relating to African-American history in Savannah. Recorded deeds of the sale of slaves are among the items displayed. (Also exhibited is a table used by Mrs. King while she lived here.)

The basement of the house contains many artifacts of 19th and 20th century domestic life in Savannah's African-American community. Slave shackles, a plow, washboards, an old wood-burning stove, and a wind-up phonograph interpret various periods of the African-American heritage.

The garden behind the house features a fountain designed by former Savannah blacksmith Ivan Bailey. The fountain is a series of symbols in the evolution of the freedom of African-Americans. Waves, an octopus, grass, and a bird take on symbolic meaning in this work of art.

MASSIE HERITAGE INTERPRETATION CENTER

207 East Gordon Street
Savannah, GA 31401
(912) 651-7022

■ ■

DAYS/HOURS OF OPERATION
Monday through Friday, 9 AM to 4 PM

ADMISSION
Voluntary donations accepted

FACILITIES
Restrooms

SPECIAL EVENTS
May Day Celebration
Georgia Heritage Celebration
Christmas Heritage Program

"That giant eye from an old building is spooky. I like all the fancy decorations that some of the downtown houses have."
Katie Ratterree, age 5

Where might one find the Parthenon in Savannah? How about the Cathedral of Notre Dame? A remnant of a Roman aqueduct? The house that Rhett Butler built for Scarlett after the Civil War? Or the gingerbread house from the tale of Hansel and Gretel?

They are all here, and the exhibits at Massie will show where to find them. In a city which holds its town plan and significant architecture in high regard, Massie should be the first stop for anyone who wants to understand the origins of Savannah's built environment. Here, three separate exhibits explain why Savannah's grid system of streets and squares is considered even today as a landmark in the history of urban design.

Massie is owned and operated by the local public school system as a resource center. It was built as a school and is known locally as Massie School. Greek revival in style, the center building was designed by the New York architect John Norris who had been hired to design the U.S. Customs House on Bay Street. The two annexes, connected to Norris' building by catwalks, were added later. The school is named for Peter Massie, whose 1841 will provided for the construction of a school for poor children.

Visitors will enjoy the exceptional exhibits which tie Savannah's many architectural styles to classical, European, and even modern architecture. Tours are self-guided and the displays are well-labeled and easy to follow. The western annex, a good place to begin, houses an exhibit showing the town plan that guided the city's development for over a century. The scale model of the historic district in the center of the room is fascinating. Children will enjoy searching for streets, museums or squares they might have passed or plan to visit.

Next stop should be the center building's main floor exhibit, which depicts the classic revival styles that predominated in Savannah's architecture during the nineteenth century. The eastern annex contains the Victorian Era exhibit. Especially appealing during the Victorian era is the abundance of decoration applied to buildings. Whether made of wood, brick or terra-cotta, buildings from this Victorian period come alive through their fanciful ornamentation. Looking for these details while touring the city makes for a lively treasure hunt.

If there is time left after seeing these three rooms, a visit to the second floor Heritage Classroom is encouraged. Most children leave this room with newfound appreciation for today's classroom!

NEGRO HERITAGE TRAIL TOUR

502 East Harris Street
Savannah, GA 31401
(912) 234-8000
Tour departs from the Savannah Visitors Center,
  301 Martin Luther King Blvd.

■ ■

DAYS/HOURS OF OPERATION
Call for schedule information

ADMISSION
$10 per adult, $5 per child

HINTS
* Allow two and one half hours
* Tourgoers are encouraged to revisit the sites pointed out
  along the way

> **"I liked the places we stopped. We heard about
> the underground railroad, and I had learned
> about that in school."**
> *Joe Ratterree, age 9*

The Negro Heritage Trail Tour is a two-hour guided bus tour that includes stops at several significant sites: Laurel Grove Cemetery, First African Baptist Church, King-Tisdell Cottage, and the Beach Institute African-American Cultural Arts Center. Leaving from the Visitors Center, the tour winds through the National Historic Landmark District and includes a section of the riverfront and Laurel Grove Cemetery. Entertaining for all ages, this tour presents many little-known facts about the African-American heritage in Savannah and their role in the rice and cotton industries. The tour also provides little known details about the African-American participation in the Revolutionary and Civil Wars. Visitors learn about the advent of slavery in Savannah and may hear for the first time that freedom could be purchased long before abolition. A stop at Laurel Grove Cemetery reveals

the burial sites of such prominent citizens as Andrew Cox Marshall and Andrew Bryant, both preachers in Savannah.

The importance of the church in the Black community begins with the First African Baptist Church, founded in 1773, as the oldest black congregation in North America. After almost a century of worshipping in various locations throughout Savannah, the congregation built the current sanctuary in 1859 of brick, later covered with stucco. Of particular interest are the African markings on the upper balcony pews. These are examples of an art form called marbleizing and depict the signatures of those who built the pews. On the main floor, the diamond-shaped patterns cut into the floor represent an African religious symbol, and they also provided ventilation for escaped slaves hidden beneath the building. Special Field Order 15, the document which called for the emancipation of all slaves, was drafted by General William T. Sherman in the Green-Meldrim House just a few blocks southeast of this church.

Two other stops on the tour, the King-Tisdell Cottage and the Beach Institute African-American Cultural Arts Center, are covered elsewhere in this book. The stops made during the tour make for a comfortable two hours with children.

THE PIRATES' HOUSE

20 East Broad Street
Savannah, GA 31401
(912) 233-5757

DAYS/HOURS OF OPERATION
7 days per week
Lunch: 11:30 AM to 2:30 PM
Afternoon desserts, coffee: 2:30 to 4:45 PM daily
Dinner: 5:30 PM to 9:45 PM
Sunday brunch buffet: 11 AM to 3 PM

COST
Children's Menu with items ranging from $.95 to $4.95
Special drinks for children

FACILITIES
Brochures
Gift shop
Handicapped access
Parking
Restrooms
Restaurant

HINTS
* Come early for lunch or dinner with children
* Birthday Parties and Special Events welcomed
* Allow 1 1/2 to 2 hours
* Plan to have dessert

"I like the pirate with the gun in his boot the best, the one named Long John Silver. I like the sign that's hanging that has a sword. I like the dungeon. The fish on the menu is my favorite. I like the pirate that talks when you push the button. And I like Blackbeard's Boot with the fruit drink and the parakeets in the bird cage."
Billy McKee, age 4

The Pirates' House has been a landmark in Savannah since 1753. Although now it functions exclusively as a restaurant with unique charm for children, it is recognized by the American Museum Society as an authentic house museum.

Originally The Pirates' House operated as an inn for seafarers and subsequently became a hang-out for pirates and sailors from Singapore to Bombay and from London to Port Said. Visitors enter the restaurant through heavy wooden doors into a dimly-lit interior. The maitre d' greets young guests with a pirate's mask which doubles as the children's menu. Seafaring pictures and paraphernalia ornament the walls and give the maze of rooms an authentic aura.

While waiting for a meal, young visitors will want to seek out Jolly George, a life-size, robotized pirate who talks and moves when children push a red button on the wall. Jolly George is placed at the top of a winding stone staircase which leads to the wine cellar, or possibly to a secret tunnel. Legend has it that sailors were shanghaied through this tunnel to the nearby Savannah River at night and brought aboard anchored ships which set sail before the hapless sailors awoke.

Older children may be inspired to read Robert Louis Stevenson's *Treasure Island*, which contains numerous references to Savannah. Indeed, Old Captain Flint may have died in an upstairs room of The Pirates' House, and some say his ghost still haunts the building.

The Pirates' House operates 15 separate dining rooms, each unique. Two of these are situated in the "Herb House," said to have been erected in 1734 and possibly the oldest building in Georgia.

RIVER STREET AND BAY STREET

"When big cargo ships come up the river, they seem so close you could reach out and touch them!"
Joe Ratterree, age 9

"I like to chase the seagulls on the sidewalk, and play in the tugboat sandbox."
Katie Ratterree, age 4

River Street, Savannah's northern boundary, has been a part of Savannah's history since James Edward Oglethorpe landed here in 1733 to establish the colony of Georgia at Savannah. The street today is far different from the rugged bluff glimpsed by the first settlers.

Rising up from the cobblestone street are tall buildings four and five stories high. The sides of the buildings which face Bay Street are only two stories high. During the 19th century, when cotton was king, the upper stories were used for conducting the business of cotton trading while the lower stories on the River Street side were used to warehouse the cotton. The walkways spanned by narrow pedestrian bridges are called Factors' Walk, referring to the business of factoring and trading that went on inside the buildings. Cotton was a major business for the port of Savannah, creating jobs and wealth for many, and River Street was the center of this activity. The stones paving River Street, called cobblestones or ballast stones, were used as ballast on empty ships entering Savannah from Europe and were left behind to make room aboard for cotton headed out of port. A striking reminder of the cotton era is the red brick and terra cotta Cotton Exchange building, between the Bull and Abercorn Street ramps.

Like much of the downtown area, River Street was largely abandoned earlier in this century. However, the preservation effort begun downtown in the 1950s caught the attention of the city, and River Street was restored in 1976 by the city of Savannah as a bicentennial project. Walkways, balustrades, landscaping and seating brought River

Street back to life. Today there is a variety of restaurants, shops, museums, and activities. Browsing, eating, shopping, exploring, and walking are just a few of the adventures that could fill several hours of time. A paddlewheel boat awaits boarding for a harbor cruise.

Beginning at either the eastern or western end of the street, visitors may start with a museum: the Ships of the Sea or the Train Museum. There are sidewalks along the buildings and storefronts and wide brick walkways closer to the river. For very young children who need to work off steam, there is a sandbox area with a small fry-sized tugboat in its center. The statue of the Waving Girl on the eastern end of the street commemorates Florence Martus, who from the 1880's to the 1930's is said to have greeted every ship entering or leaving the port by waving a white cloth during the day and a lantern at night. Several riverboat tours are available here. At times, large cruise ships dock along River Street. Often a huge container ship will pass by, stirring visions of stowaways and travels to far off places and leaving even grown-ups agog at the size of these vessels.

Few children (or parents, for that matter) will be able to resist exploring the ramps and stone stairways that lead up to the Bay Street level. There are as many landmarks and sights of interest here as there are down below on River Street. From City Hall, with its distinctive gold dome, east toward Emmet Park there are fountains, cannons, lions, bells, and monuments worth investigating. Visitors can get back to River Street by walking down the cobblestone streets or stone stairways accessed from Factors' Walk.

RIVER STREET TRAIN MUSEUM

315 West River Street
Savannah, GA 31401
(912) 233-6175

■■

DAYS/HOURS OF OPERATION
Monday - Saturday, 11 AM to 6 PM
Sunday, 1 PM to 6 PM

ADMISSION
$1.50 per adult
$.50 per child, ages 5 - 12
Children under 5, free with an accompanying adult

FACILITIES
Drink & snack machines
Gift Shop
Restroom

HINTS
* Allow 30 minutes
* Reservations required for groups
* Discounts available for groups

*"I've never seen so many trains before. The whole
room is full of them."*
Joe Ratterree, age 9

Located at the far western end of River Street, the River Street
Train Museum is a combination of retail shop and model train exhibit.
The museum is a large room with a 16 x 28 foot track layout in its
center. On the walls surrounding the layout are displays of model trains
dating from the 1930's. Several different gauges are represented here,
including the Spirit of '76, a bicentennial edition in which each state
has a car attached to the engine in order of its admission to the Union.
The colorful decorative details of the train displays are appealing, but

when the guide cranks up the trains in the center layout, the action begins. Whistles, smoke, and chug-a-chug noises fill the room as several trains take off on concentric tracks. Most of the trains on exhibit are freight trains, with piggyback freight cars that are offloaded by "huge" cranes in much the same fashion that real offloading occurs just upriver at the Georgia Ports Authority.

With good timing or a little bit of luck, a visit to the Train Museum may coincide with a run of the River Street Rambler along the track that is in the middle of River Street. This engine, dressed up in bright colors for the company on River Street, is owned by the Norfolk-Southern Railroad and is used to pull cars between the industry clusters on either end of the street.

SAVANNAH HISTORY MUSEUM

Managed by The Coastal Heritage Society
303 Martin Luther King Jr. Blvd.
Savannah, GA 31401
(912) 238-1779

■ ■

DAYS/HOURS OF OPERATION
Weekdays 8:30 AM to 5 PM
Weekends 9 AM to 5 PM
Closed Thanksgiving, Christmas, New Year's Day

ADMISSION
$3 per adult
$2.50 senior citizens
$1.75 per child 6 - 12; children under 6, free
$10 family rate
Special student and group rates upon request
Tax not included in these prices

FACILITIES
Gift Shop
Handicapped access
Parking
Restrooms
Deli Bar
Visitors Center

HINTS
* Allow an hour
* Check on movie show times; "Siege of Savannah" shown only
  twice per day
* Special parties catered. Call for information

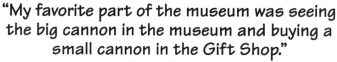

"My favorite part of the museum was seeing
the big cannon in the museum and buying a
small cannon in the Gift Shop."
Billy McKee, age 5

What was once a bustling passenger depot for the Central of Georgia Railway is now the Savannah History Museum. The Museum opened in 1990 to preserve and display Savannah's cultural and historic heritage. Many visitors to Savannah make this their first stop because of its location next to the Savannah Visitors Center.

The Savannah History Museum building dates from 1860, when it operated to serve the railroad. That function ended in 1971. In 1977, the old depot was designated a National Historic Landmark. But even before the railroad depot was built, this site was the location of a major Revolutionary War battle.

On October 9, 1779, over 7000 men from three continents (Europe, North America, and Africa) fought for possession of Savannah. Here American and French soldiers fought British soldiers in a bloody battle that left over 1000 men wounded or dead. At the Battle of Spring Hill, known as the Siege of Savannah, the American soldiers suffered a crushing defeat at the hand of the British. Using lead soldiers, local historian Preston Russell has recreated the battle scene inside the museum.

The museum houses two theatres. In the first, visitors can see "Savannah the Survivor," an 18-minute film which covers Savannah's history from its founding in 1733 to the present day. Narrated by the impersonation of James Edward Oglethorpe, founder of Savannah, the film is shown at regular intervals in a comfortable, colonial-style theater. Another film, "Siege of Savannah," is shown only twice a day in a stand-up theater with a large, dramatic screen.

Children will enjoy seeing a real steam locomotive built in 1890 for the Central of Georgia Railroad. Other exhibits include Civil War artifacts, Native-American artifacts, soldiers' uniforms, maps and prints of Old Savannah, river and sea exhibits, a cotton gin, real bales of cotton, and an impressive collection of documents on Georgia's African-American military history. Stacks of cannon balls and artillery projectiles will attract younger children. These Confederate projectiles were recovered from the *CSS Georgia*, a floating battery built in 1862 to defend the Savannah River from the advance of General Sherman's troops. Confederate soldiers sunk the *CSS Georgia* to prevent Union troops from capturing the battery, and the ship still rests on the bottom of the Savannah River near Fort Jackson.

SAVANNAH NATIONAL WILDLIFE REFUGE

Owned and managed by U.S. Fish and Wildlife Service
1000 Business Center Parkway
Parkway Business Center, Suite 10
Savannah, GA 31405
(912) 652-4415
Refuge Location:
Highway 17, near the Houlihan Bridge

■ ■

DAYS/HOURS OF OPERATION
Daylight use only
Closed all Federal holidays

ADMISSION
Free

FACILITIES
Parking
Picnic area
Restrooms
Trails

HINTS
* Bug spray is a must during warm weather!
* Do not bring pets
* Stay on cleared dikes and paths
* Bring binoculars

"We liked seeing the owl on her nest, but we didn't get too close, and we liked seeing the alligators."
Mary Ellen McKee, age13; Tom McKee, age10 and Billy McKee, age 5

The Savannah National Wildlife Refuge is a short drive from downtown Savannah, straddling the border of Georgia and South Carolina. For nature enthusiasts, this is a delightful respite from the urban environment. Birds and alligators are abundant in the refuge, which covers 25,608 acres of freshwater marsh, tidal rivers and creeks, and bottomland hardwood swamps.

This wildlife refuge was established in 1927, encompassing as many as 13 former rice plantations. The 3000 acres of freshwater impoundments are maintained in the same manner as they were when rice was grown in the late 18th and 19th centuries. A series of "trunks" or flood - gates allow water from the Savannah River to enter at high tide or exit at low tide. Tidal power and trunks made of creosoted pine offer the most efficient method of controlling water levels in the refuge, even in the late twentieth century.

The best way to see the refuge is to begin at the main entrance and follow the four-mile Laurel Hill Drive around the eastern part of the refuge. This driving tour is a quick way for children to see the refuge, with stops for short hikes or picnicking. There is lots to see from the car, particularly in fall, winter, and spring. A pair of bald eagles frequents the refuge in late winter, and a pair of great horned owls have become refuge mascots because of a favorite nesting spot right at the beginning of Laurel Hill Drive.

Wonderful live oak trees border the small rise at the entrance of the refuge, which once was a part of the Laurel Hill Plantation home. The only restrooms in the refuge area are at this entrance.

Laurel Hill Drive wanders along earthen dikes built two centuries ago which separate the freshwater impoundments. On the right of the drive is the Savannah River and the very visible signs of Savannah's major industries. Driving further, this urban view is obscured by forest, and visitors are surrounded by the sights and sounds of the refuge.

Wading birds, shorebirds, waterfowl, hawks, owls, the rare swallow-tailed kite, the bald eagle, and even the peregrine falcon are possible sightings in the over 260 species of birds that regularly visit the refuge. Alligators, turtles, otters, snakes, or a mink might be seen in the water or on the banks of the ponds and creeks. Deer, raccoons, bobcats, and opossums are also residents here, although they are very shy and usually difficult to spot.

Guided tours are available with advance arrangements. Because of limited Fish and Wildlife staff, volunteers regularly lead tours through the refuge, hiking Cistern Trail and pointing out difficult-to-see wildlife. Fishing is permitted from February/March through October 25 with Georgia or South Carolina fishing licenses (obtained through the refuge office). Limited hunting seasons in October, November, and March are permitted, and during these times certain areas of the refuge are off-limits to visitors. Restrictions are also placed on the area north of U. S. Highway 17 to protect wintering waterfowl from November 1 to March 15. Parts of the refuge are accessible only by boat or on foot. There are 25 miles of dikes for hardy hikers or bikers, but this is not recommended for young children.

The refuge is not only a haven for wildlife, but also a retreat for people who will enjoy glimpsing life on the undeveloped side of the Savannah River.

WORD SEARCH

```
C D X S U P Q A N F Z O L M Y X O
B E T F Z A M Y L P C N D F J G T
G A C H J I K O Q R T Y F T V S T
Z G O L M Z A L L I G A T O R Z E
D L K N Q O R B S P X R A W K B R
D E E R A T N I K B E H J L N Q Z
J B Q M Z Y S T C D N O K M F F N
A Z S L F D B K O E J B S N A K E
N T I D E S C F H I L O P R L Q B
Z T U N B O P Q C F D B G J C H X
X L M R Z C E G O D U C K I O L P
A Z B Y T D X C V L T A M U N Z V
V N U S R L K A D B Z T X C R P T
R P Z D H G E K U N V S W A M P O
```

TIDE	ALLIGATOR	RICE	OTTER
SNAKE	DEER	FALCON	
EAGLE	OWL	TURTLE	
BOBCAT	DUCK	SWAMP	

answer on page 106

SAVANNAH'S SQUARES AND FORSYTH PARK

━━━━━━━━━━━━━━━━━━━━━━━━━━━━━━━━━━━━

"We always have an adventure when we go downtown. Every square has something different."
Joe Ratterree, age 8

"My favorite place is the big playground at Forsyth Park. The slides there are very tall. I also like the square by the college, where I like to get something to eat and drink."
Katie Ratterree, age 5

A walk through Savannah's historic district is a walk back in time. Whether strolling along the bluff overlooking the Savannah River or resting on a park bench under the canopy of centuries-old oaks, visitors will fall captive to the relaxed pace of an earlier time. Certainly Savannah's original town plan, brought by founder James Edward Oglethorpe in 1733, defines the pace. The crown jewels of the town plan are Savannah's squares, oases of calm in the fast lane of city life. Of the 24 squares that were laid out between 1733 and 1856, 21 remain, quietly imposing a sense of order and harmony within the 2.2 square mile historic district. Around each square there are shops, schools, homes, museums, restaurants, churches and businesses in restored nineteenth century buildings that narrowly escaped demolition during the 1940's and 1950's.

A key to understanding the town plan is to remember the function of the squares as gathering places for the surrounding homes and businesses. In the 18th century, fear of attack from any number of enemies was very real, and the squares were places where colonists could gather for protection. They were also used to corral animals. The four large lots facing east and west on each square, called trust lots, were reserved for buildings of prominence, such as churches, civic buildings, and later for residences of prominent citizens. The four lots on the north and south sides of each square were called tything lots, because they were each divided into 10 lots intended for homes. Therefore, each square was the center of a cozy neighborhood called a ward, and the whole system of wards and squares was continued until 1851.

There are several tour companies in Savannah that give a more complete story of Savannah's history, architecture and the preservation movement. The Massie Heritage Interpretation Center housed in the Massie School building on Calhoun Square provides a good overview of the Historic District. The following paragraphs describe a few squares that have special appeal for children. All of the squares have shade and benches, and most are visited by pigeons and squirrels who adore peanuts. A bag of nuts may allow a new friendship to blossom!

Most of the squares feature a focal point in their centers, usually a fountain or a monument, sometimes both.

JOHNSON SQUARE, the first square laid out in 1733, is downtown Savannah's financial center and keeps a lively pace. Located here is Christ Episcopal Church, the first church in Georgia. On certain days of the week, musical performances take place in the square around lunchtime, drawing a wide array of people to hear everything from jazz to string quartets. Cart vendors offer fast food a la historic district; traditional fast food restaurants are not located in the historic district. In the center of Johnson Square is a monument to Nathanael Greene, who served as Chief of Staff to George Washington in the American Revolution, and who was given Mulberry Grove plantation near Savannah in appreciation for his military service. There are two fountains in this square, where wishes can be made with the toss of a coin.

WRIGHT SQUARE, at one time called Court House Square, is home to two major government buildings. It was named for Sir James Wright, the last Royal Governor of Georgia. In its center is a monument to William Washington Gordon who was mayor of Savannah and the grandfather of Juliette Gordon Low, founder of the Girl Scouts. In one corner of the square is a large granite boulder which was placed to honor Yamacraw Indian Chief Tomochichi, whose friend-ship was invaluable to Oglethorpe in settling the colony. Local tra-dition holds that if one walks around the boulder three times, knocks on it, and asks Tomochichi what he is doing, he'll say nothing!

CHIPPEWA SQUARE features in its center a statue of Gen-eral James Edward Oglethorpe, founder of the colony of Georgia at Savannah on February 12, 1733. The statue was created by artist Daniel Chester French. It is said that Oglethorpe faces south because that is the direction from which the colonial enemy, the Spanish armies in Florida, would have come.

MADISON SQUARE is probably Savannah's most diverse with homes, a church, a hotel, several shops, a college, and the Green-Meldrim House which served as headquarters for General Sherman during the Union occupation of Savannah. There is always a high level of activity here. In the center is a statue of Revolutionary War hero Sergeant William Jasper, commander of Fort Moultrie who was killed in the attack on Savannah, October 9, 1779. The statue shows Jasper rescuing his company's flag. On the southern end of the square are two cannons which are irresistible for climbing and unbeatable for photo opportunities.

MONTEREY SQUARE features Savannah's finest assortment of ornamental ironwork. Just about every shape, size and configura-tion can be found on the balconies and high stoops of the homes on this square. The pelican newel posts at 4 West Taylor are of great interest to children. Guarding the entry to the house, each pelican holds in its raised claw a pebble, which, if the pelican fell asleep, would fall to the ground, making a noise that would wake the pelican to resume its sentinel duties. Pencils, crayons and paper may come in handy to draw some of the patterns found in the ironwork.

FORSYTH PARK, laid out in 1851 and named for Governor John Forsyth, is a favorite for walkers and joggers. The cast iron foun-

tain in its center, erected in 1858, is surrounded by signature bricks which represent names of those citizens who assisted in the restoration of the fountain in 1988. The northern section of the park is like a giant maze. Sidewalks wind through landscaped sections planted with azaleas and many species of trees and shrubbery. There are two playgrounds here and large expanses of open areas used as playing fields for rugby, soccer, and frisbee. A wading pool near the playgrounds is inviting in the summer, and the shadier spots are used for Art In the Park and other community-sponsored programs. The two

structures near the playgrounds were built after World War I as dummy forts for military training. One of these was converted into a fragrant garden for the blind. The other serves as a backdrop for plays and other events. In the southern section of the park are two statues, one a monument in sandstone honoring the Confederate dead, and the other a bronze statue commemorating those who served in the Spanish-American War. Tennis and basketball courts are located at this end of the park. At least once a year, the Savannah Symphony Orchestra holds an outdoor concert in Forsyth. Other festivals and celebrations such as Earth Day and the Jazz Festival, draw people to Forsyth Park. Throughout the year, this park is an inviting spot for picnics.

Across Drayton Street from Forsyth Park is the **CANDLER OAK**, the largest live oak tree in the Historic District, estimated to be between 200 and 300 years old. This tree is protected by a conservation easement held by the Savannah Tree Foundation.

COLONIAL CEMETERY is located at the intersection of Abercorn Street and Oglethorpe Avenue. In earlier centuries it served as a burial ground for both the parish of Christ Church and the city. At the end of its use as a cemetery, its maintenance was turned over to the Park and Tree Commission. Today it is enjoyed as a passive park. There are some lovely old gravestones here, and markers identify well-known names in Savannah's and Georgia's history. At the southern end of the cemetery is a playground. Across Abercorn Street is a rather large fire station in an older building. Most young children enjoy seeing the enormous trucks, and the local firemen enjoy showing them around.

SAVANNAH VISITORS CENTER

301 Martin Luther King Blvd.
P. O. Box 1628
Savannah, GA 31402-1628
(912) 944-0456

DAYS/HOURS OF OPERATION
7 Days a week, 9 AM to 5 PM
Includes all holidays

ADMISSION
Free

FACILITIES
Gift Shop
Information
Parking
Restrooms

HINTS
* Begin Savannah visit here
* Combine with visits to nearby Historic Railroad Shops and
  Savannah History Museum

"I liked to play with the computer."
Billy McKee, age 5

The Savannah Visitors Center, managed by the Savannah Area
Convention & Visitors Bureau, is located in the restored passenger
depot of the Central of Georgia Railway, built in 1860. Sharing the
building with the Savannah History Museum, the Visitors Center is
a great place for the newcomer in Savannah to begin. Staffed with
personnel willing to offer assistance, the Visitors Center has racks of
brochures, complimentary maps, restaurant guides, and a courtesy
phone for reservations at a number of Bed and Breakfast Inns. It is also
the originating point for all trolley or bus tours and provides a com-
puterized "Touch Me Information System."

The enclosed atrium, located between the Visitors Center and the Savannah History Museum, offers tables and chairs and access to refreshments at the snack bar. Located in the atrium are large, painted murals depicting Savannah's founders and influential citizens, historic scenes, and a model of the Great Savannah Exposition in 1985.

The Visitors Center provides an opportunity for a general orientation to Savannah with generous parking facilities. A little pre-planning here will help visitors make the most of their time.

SHIPS OF THE SEA MUSEUM

503 East River Street (lower level)
504 East Bay Street (upper level)
Savannah, GA 31401
(912) 232-1511

■ ■

DAYS/HOURS OF OPERATION
Daily, 10 AM to 5 PM
Closed St. Patrick's Day, Thanksgiving, Christmas Day, and
  New Year's Day

ADMISSION
$3 per adult
$1.50 per child, 7 - 12
Free, children under 7
$1 per child, school groups and scouts

FACILITIES
Gift Shop
Restrooms
Water fountain

HINTS
* Allow one hour for visit
* Preschoolers need to be watched carefully

"The ships are remarkable. I liked the ships in the bottle.
There was a cannon too. It's on the river bluff and you
can see the big ships go by."
Tom McKee, Jr., age 9

There are several reasons to visit the Ships of the Sea Museum,
located on historic Factors' Walk on the Savannah River. Children will
be fascinated by the maritime history chronicled through models of
Viking ships, Chinese war ships, the Mayflower, the S. S. Savannah,
and many others. The collection of over 75 ships in a bottle, nautical

prints and paintings, scrimshaw, and an exhibit on cotton and the cotton gin are lessons in themselves as visitors explore the four floors of this historic building.

Built on the Savannah River bluff 200 years ago, the upper two stories of the Museum originally functioned as offices for ship owners, architects, customs officials, and brokers. From these upper stories today, visitors have a panoramic view of the Savannah River, the main artery of transportation during the 18th and 19th centuries. There is the possibility of glimpsing a modern day tanker or container ship as it carefully navigates the river past the museum. The lower two levels of the building were utilized as warehouses, and children will enjoy climbing from one level to another. There is no elevator, so those who have difficulty climbing will need to remain either on the bottom level, which is entered from River Street, or on the top level, which is entered from Bay Street.

The cannons, the smells and sounds of the river, the old casks and trunks, and the impressive models of ships all evoke the atmosphere of a port city. This glimpse of Savannah's maritime past offers a nice contrast to the graceful new cable bridge, easily seen from all levels of the Museum, spanning the river that brought the first settlers to Savannah.

TELFAIR MUSEUM OF ART

121 Barnard Street
Savannah, GA 31401
(912) 232-1177

- -

DAYS/HOURS OF OPERATION
Tuesday - Saturday, 10 AM - 5 PM
Sunday 2 PM to 5 PM (admission free)

ADMISSION
Members Free
$3 per adult
$1 per student/senior citizen
$.50 per child, ages 6 - 12
Free to all on Sundays

FACILITIES
Elevator
Handicapped access
Limited parking with pass available inside
Restrooms

SPECIAL EVENTS
Free Family Sundays
Lecture Series
Free Docent-Guided Tours on Sundays

HINTS
* Call about special programs and exhibits

> "I have a favorite painting here, a little girl
> in a room with an open door behind her.
> My grandma takes me here."
> *Katie Ratterree, age 4*

> "I like the statue downstairs with the snakes."
> *Joe Ratterree, age 9*

The Telfair is Savannah's art museum, located in the Telfair Academy building. In fact, it is the oldest art museum in Georgia, having opened in 1886. The history of the building predates the museum, for William Jay designed this mansion for Alexander Telfair in 1818, and it served as a home until Margaret Telfair's will decreed in 1875 that it be used as an art museum. After several years of major additions and renovations, the Telfair mansion opened in 1886 as an art museum. Today, the Telfair boasts an impressive collection of American and European paintings of the late nineteenth and early twentieth centuries, as well as sculpture and decorative arts.

Before entering the museum, visitors are greeted by a welcoming committee consisting of Phidias, Rubens, Raphael, Michelangelo and Rembrandt. These statues were commissioned by the first director for the museum in the 1880's. Once inside, it is fun to imagine what it must have been like to enter here when it was a home. On either side of the huge marbled foyer are rooms befitting the mansion. On the right is a double drawing room. On the left are the Octagon Room and Dining Room, each featuring a unique wall treatment.

The stairs lead up to the Rotunda where paintings from the permanent collection are exhibited. Around the room are murals commissioned for the museum depicting representatives of the arts: Praxiteles, a Greek sculptor; Iktinus, the architect of the Parthenon; Appeles, a Greek painter; and Durer, a German printmaker representing the graphic arts. The paintings in the Rotunda date from 1870 through 1900. There is a wide variety of subject matter in these paintings, and parents will want to point out items of interest that young eyes might miss. Another flight up leads to four galleries where changing exhibits are displayed. A phone call in advance will provide information on these exhibits or special programs. Large banners hung on the front of the building also announce current exhibits.

Following the steps back down all the way to the bottom will lead visitors to the sculpture gallery, aptly named for the statues located here. On the walls are more paintings from the permanent collection, dating after 1870. There is also a nineteenth-century kitchen gallery on this level.

The Telfair offers several programs for groups of children. One of the most popular programs is the Free Family Sunday series, a quarterly offering of hands-on activities and demonstrations related to various exhibits. Every child leaves one of these programs with something he or she has made. During the summer the Treasure Trunks program brings the museum into the city parks and squares. Information on all of these activities is available through a phone call.

Future plans for the Telfair include a new building on the same square to provide additional exhibition space. The museum owns a large collection of paintings and needs more space in which to display them. The new building will also house educational spaces including an interactive gallery, classrooms, and an auditorium.

MRS. WILKES' BOARDING HOUSE

107 West Jones Street
Savannah, GA 31401
(912) 232-5997

■ ■

DAYS/HOURS OF OPERATION
Monday - Friday for Breakfast, 8 AM to 9 AM and
Lunch 11 AM to 3 PM
Usually closed the first two weeks in July

COST
$5 Breakfast
$8 Lunch

FACILITIES
Restaurant
Restrooms

HINTS
* Allow 15 to 45 minutes for waiting in line
* Bring an umbrella in case it rains, as the wait is outside
* Go early with small children

"This is my favorite place to eat in town!"
Mary Ellen McKee, age 12

Standing in line may be a test of patience, but the meal here is always worth the wait. Children will enjoy the family-style seating, ten to twelve at a table in true boarding house fashion. With up to seventeen different dishes at lunchtime, even the pickiest eaters will find something to enjoy. Homestyle, southern cooking is Mrs. Wilkes' specialty with platters and bowls heaped high with mashed potatoes, fried chicken, fish, rice, gravy, dressing, all sorts of vegetables, biscuits, dessert, and more.

Mrs. Wilkes' Dining Room is located on the ground floor of a historic paired residence on West Jones Street. Built in 1870, the house was bought and restored by Mr. and Mrs. Wilkes in 1965, the first home to be restored in an area that was fast becoming a slum. Built of Savannah grey brick, the house features double curving steps and cast iron trim.

How did Mrs. Wilkes come to operate such a successful dining room? Her story begins during World War II when the U. S. government bought her farm in Vidalia for an airstrip. She moved to Savannah and took a room in Mrs. Dixon's Boarding House on Jones Street. Shortly afterwards, she began helping Mrs. Dixon with the cooking for her boarders. Eventually, Mrs. Wilkes ran the Dining Room and the Boarding House, which led to ownership.

For many years Mrs. Wilkes fed only her boarders, but the demand for her cooking led her to open to a very limited public. Today, Mrs. Wilkes serves up to 250 people a day and enjoys an international reputation as a famous southern cook. She has been featured in magazines such as *Esquire*, *TIME*, *Brown's Guide To Georgia*, and *Redbook*.

Mrs. Wilkes' award-winning dining room has been family operated since the 1940s with the stated secret, "Never serve food that has not been sampled before leaving the kitchen."

EAST SAVANNAH, ISLANDS, AND TYBEE

1. Fort Pulaski National Monument
2. McQueen's Island Trail/Tybee Rails to Trails
3. Oatland Island Education Center
4. Old Fort Jackson
5. Tybee Island Marine Science Center Foundation, Inc.
6. Tybee Lighthouse
7. Tybee Museum

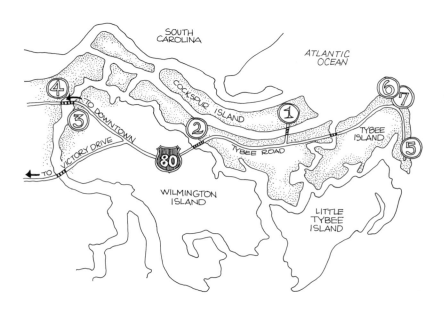

FORT PULASKI NATIONAL MONUMENT

U. S. Department of the Interior, National Park Service
P. O. Box 30757
Cockspur Island
Savannah, GA 31410-0757
(912) 786-5787

- -

DAYS/HOURS OF OPERATION
Open daily except December 25,
8:30 AM to 5:30 PM
Hours may be extended during Summer; call for details.

ADMISSION
$2 per adult
Children 16 and under, free
$4 Maximum per immediate family

FACILITIES
Boat launching ramp
Bookstore
Fishing
Handicapped access; wheelchair available for use; audiotape for
 blind; transcripts for hearing impaired
Parking
Picnic area
Restrooms
Trails
Visitor Center
Water fountains

SPECIAL EVENTS
April-Siege and Reduction Weekend, usually between
 April 1 and 10
July 4th, Meridian Musket Salute
August 25th (National Parks Day), Special Programs
Labor Day Weekend, Encampment

Weekend before Christmas, Confederate Nog Party of 1861,
Candlelight Tour of Fort.
Reservations required.

HINTS

* Picnic (allowed only in picnic area)
* Bug Spray
* Comfortable shoes
* Allow 1 to 2 hours for fort tour; 3 to 4 hours for fort plus picnic and trail
* The fort was built for war, not safety. Watch your step and stay off mounds and topmost walls.
* Birthday parties and special groups welcome; advance notice requested.

"I liked best the draw-bridge, the cannons upstairs and downstairs, and the water fountain. The fort is neat. The fort men, the benches, and oh yeah, the moat. And the draw-bridge you can go across, it can wind up."
Billy McKee, age 4

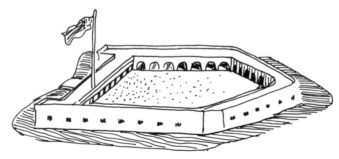

This castle-like fort, completed in 1847, will capture the imagination of children of all ages. The fort took 18 years to build. In the early part of his career, Robert E. Lee, working for the Corps of Engineers, was second in command in overseeing the construction of the fort. It was Lee who designated the specific site for Fort Pulaski and who developed the dike and drainage system for the fort. General Lee returned to Fort Pulaski during the Civil War to command the Confederate defense of the fort.

Considered at the time of construction to be a state-of-the-art facility, Fort Pulaski's vulnerability to the all-new rifled cannon marked the end of an era in fort construction. The pentagon-shaped fort still retains its original character and the visitor will want to allow plenty of time to explore.

Located on Cockspur Island, about 15 miles east of Savannah, Fort Pulaski became a national monument in 1924. It is named for Count Casimir Pulaski, a Polish hero who fought in the American Revolution and who was mortally wounded in the 1779 Battle of Savannah. The opportunities for a day's adventure include a nature walk, picnic, a visit to the bookstore, history lessons, and imaginative adventure.

The fort's impressive masonry structure is built of 25 million bricks. The moat surrounding the fort holds the promise of a few wild alligators, and two draw-bridges give Fort Pulaski fairy-tale security. Take time to explore the maze of underground tunnels, rooms and niches after crossing the first draw-bridge. Just past the second draw-bridge, examine the massive doors made of Georgia heart pine.

Once inside the fort, there are two levels around a large quadrangle with a grassy parade ground in the center. Cannons, a prison, soldiers' quarters with beds and mattresses stuffed with straw all portray the life of the soldier. From the upper level of the fort, visitors can view the mouth of the Savannah River as it enters the Atlantic Ocean. On a clear day, Daufuskie, Hilton Head, and Tybee Islands are also visible. Visitors should watch children on the upper level of the fort, for there are no rails or safety guards to prevent a fall.

Benches on the parade grounds are shaded by two large pecan trees. Interpretive programs are given here at announced times. Close by are restrooms, water fountains, and a cannon. This is a wonderful place for children to play after touring the fort.

The visitor's center is a combination bookstore, museum, and information center. Maps, daily information on programs, and a 15-minute video help to orient the visitor. The shop has an unusual array of Confederate flags and a number of books about the Confederacy, forts, and history.

A hiking trail (.6 mile) leads from the parking lot to the picnic area. The trail is easy to follow with interpretive signs along the way and travels through woods and open, grassy areas where deer might be visible. Snakes and alligators are possibilities, and it is best to stay on the trail. Three detours at the outset of the trail include the old North Pier, Battery Hambright, and Wesley Memorial. The picnic area, shaded by pine and palmetto trees, is clean and well-kept with over a dozen picnic tables. Parking, restrooms, trash cans, and the occasional river breeze make this area a perfect picnic spot.

MCQUEENS ISLAND TRAIL/ TYBEE RAILS TO TRAILS

Managed by the Chatham County Department of Parks,
   Recreation and Cultural Affairs
U. S. Highway 80 East
Savannah, GA 31401
(912) 652-6786, 652-6780

■ ■

DAYS/HOURS OF OPERATION
Daily, sunup to sundown

ADMISSION
Free

FACILITIES
Exercise stations
Handicapped access
Parking
Picnic facilities
Restrooms

HINTS
* Bring bug spray
* Wear comfortable shoes
* Plan a picnic
* Be alert for snakes

"It's neat, but hot (in the summer)!"
Billy McKee, age 5

   A testimony to the success of volunteers and the commitment of
the Chatham County Department of Parks, Recreation and Cultural
Affairs, this six-and-a-half mile long trail is a delightful way to exercise while enjoying the abundant wildlife and scenic views. Following
an abandoned railway corridor, this multi-purpose trail is designed for

cycling, jogging, walking, and camping. There are nine fitness stations along the scenic and historic trail.

Located on the railway line which once connected Savannah to Tybee Island, this line was abandoned in the 1930's due to the popularity of car travel. The trail itself is part of a national system of trails known as the Conversion of Rails to Trails, and this organization designated the McQueens Island Trail one of America's first 500 Rail Trails.

The trail runs west to east from Elba Creek to the Lazaretto Creek Boat Ramp Park. Children should be accompanied by adults along the entire length of the trail because there are rattlesnakes present in the area. A 175-foot long fishing pier with parking in the South Channel holds the promise of flounder or trout for supper.

OATLAND ISLAND EDUCATION CENTER

Owned and managed by the Savannah/Chatham
  Board of Education
711 Sandtown Road
Savannah, GA 31411
(912) 897-3773

DAYS/HOURS OF OPERATION
Monday - Friday, 8:30 AM to 5 PM

ADMISSION
Cash donations accepted

FACILITIES
Parking
Picnic area
Restrooms
Trails

SPECIAL EVENTS
October through May, Second Saturday special programs
November, Annual Cane Grinding and Craft Festival
Annual Sheep Shearing

HINTS
* Allow at least 3 hours to include a picnic
* May be tiring for younger children. Bring stroller or baby carrier.
* Bring bug spray!
* Bring extra drinks, snacks
* Gates are locked at 5 PM

"I like the way Oatland makes the animals feel at home."
Marianne Lee, age 12

"I liked seeing especially the bald eagle and the huge alligator."
Billy McKee, age 5

Oatland Island Education Center is a unique and special experience for children of all ages. Operating as an environmental education center, Oatland is maintained by the Savannah/Chatham County Public School System. It is not a zoo, but it does provide the opportunity to see native animals and birds of coastal Georgia in their natural habitat. Some of these animals are threatened or endangered; some have been injured and cannot be returned to the wild.

Oatland Island with its 175-acres is committed to wildlife conservation and educating children about coastal Georgia's native animals. The Center was awarded a conservation citation by Mutual of Omaha's Wildlife Heritage Trust in 1994.

Following the nature trail will give the visitor a full view of Oatland Island's delightful animal experiences. Trail guides are available in the Main Building. Trails are well marked and well traveled, with educational markers at the various animal habitats.

Highlights of the trail include close-up views of a pair of endangered bald eagles, a walk-in shore-bird aviary, and the opportunity to view the rare Florida panther. Other animals at Oatland which are rarely seen in the wild by humans include gray wolves, black bear, red fox, bobcats, and other small mammals. A pair of wood bison are some of Oatland's newest residents which nowadays can be seen only in national parks or on private lands. Three different types of owls - the great horned owl, the barred owl, and the barn owl - will engage the visitor in a staring contest.

The barnyard area portrays animal life on a farm with a pig, cow, chickens, goats, rabbits, sheep, and turkeys. Tucked away in a clearing in the forest is the Heritage Homesite area where two restored 1835 log cabins provide a rustic spot for educational programs and the annual fall crafts festival and cane grinding.

Oatland Island is open for public and private schools as well as for the general public. Guided tours and special programs are available with advance reservations. The animals and birds in their natural habitats have much to teach visitors of all ages in Oatland's unique learning environment.

OLD FORT JACKSON

1 Fort Jackson Road
Savannah, GA 31404
(912) 232-3945

- -

DAYS/HOURS OF OPERATION
7 days per week, 9 AM to 5 PM
Closed Thanksgiving, Christmas, New Year's Day

ADMISSION
$2.65 per adult
$2.12 per child, students, senior citizens, military
Ages 5 and under, free

FACILITIES
Baby changing station
Drink machines
Gift shop
Handicapped access
Leashed pets allowed
Parking
Picnic area
Restrooms
Shelter
Visitors Center

HINTS
* Bug Spray
* Take a picnic
* Allow one and one half hours
* Great place for parties. A cannon-firing is a hallmark of planned
  parties.

**"This is one of my favorite places to visit because you
can run around and play pretend war."**
Joe Ratterree, age 8

> **"My brother had his birthday party here once, and we dressed up like soldiers. Sometimes a huge ship comes by the fort."**
> *Katie Ratterree, age 4*

Fort Jackson is located three miles from Savannah at a point on the Savannah River where all channels converge. Every ship entering or leaving the port of Savannah passes here. Today, this almost surely guarantees a glimpse of a huge container ship. A century and a half earlier, however, this strategic location had great potential for coastal defense. This is exactly what President Jefferson had in mind in 1808 when construction of the fort was begun on what was formerly a colonial brickyard and Revolutionary War earthworks. The Fort as it is seen today was built in two major phases, the second being completed in time for the Civil War.

The Orientation Center near the parking lot is the old depot building for the Tybee Railroad. Formerly located closer to Savannah, the structure was moved to the Fort in 1989. Here visitors purchase their admission tickets. The gift shop is worth a stop on the way out. Visitors walk along a Belgian block pathway to the river where markers explain the historic events that occurred on or near the site. The large open area to the right is the site of former rice fields.

Another path leads to the fort where visitors enter in nineteenth-century fashion via a drawbridge. Cannon-firing demonstrations take place in the center area which is flanked on both sides by barracks foundations and covered pavilions. A brick stairway leads up to a parapet where a large cannon is located. The sweeping view from here illustrates why this site was so attractive for river defense. Beneath the parapet an enclosed exhibit area features many displays that interpret the fort's history. Children enjoy wandering through the tunnels and alcoves inside. The first stop should be the small room with an audio-visual presentation which is self- activated. This 20-minute overview is most informative. Military uniforms, weapons from various eras, and collections of artifacts are displayed in the alcoves which provide structural support for the weight of the parapet overhead. Of particular interest are two models of Fort Jackson, one circa 1812 and the other, 1864. These clarify the phases of the construction that took place between 1808 and 1864.

TYBEE ISLAND MARINE SCIENCE CENTER FOUNDATION

P. O. Box 1879
Tybee Island, GA 31328
(912) 786-5917
Located at the end of 15th Street and 16th Street, on the beach

■■

DAYS/HOURS OF OPERATION
Daily 9 AM to 4 PM, summer only

ADMISSION
Free; donations accepted

FACILITIES
Restrooms

SPECIAL EVENTS
Art displays
Beach walks
Sea camps
Evening programs

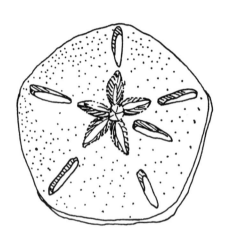

> "My favorite thing about this visit was seeing
> the sharks' teeth."
> *Ben Beason, age 14*

    Opened in 1988, the Tybee Island Marine Science Center offers a quick overview of marine life on and near the beach. Five saltwater aquariums provide close-up views of what is swimming in the ocean just outside the door. A touch-tank encourages curious hands to pick up and examine live whelks, conchs, hermit crabs, and sea anemones.

    Further into the Science Center, a large display of southeastern shells rests in sand, each grouping of shells well-labeled. There is a microscope for the curious who want to examine the shells in more detail. Displays of the marsh and the beach, a small sea-turtle exhibit, a crab trap, and some preserved sea life all create the atmosphere of the science lab.

Rows of shark's teeth embedded in the opened skeleton jaws of several sharks impress even the youngest visitor. Whales are rare, but sometimes happen into the waters off Tybee. A few large vertebrae of a Humpback whale are displayed as well as information on the dolphin, a volunteer-driven dolphin monitoring study. Charts and information on Gray's Reef, a large Marine National Sanctuary located off-shore, show the many varieties of marine life that inhabit the Reef.

What can be seen in the Science Center is just a surface glimpse of all the many activities which occur behind the scenes. Before planning a trip, a call ahead to the Center will provide information on scheduled beach walks, special evening programs, sea camps during the summer, special displays in the upstairs gallery, staff lectures, and videos.

The Marine Science Center is located on the beach between 15th and 16th Streets. Its front door faces the ocean, inviting beachcombers to bring in their "finds" for identification. Immediately beside the Center is an all-day parking lot equipped with a fresh-water shower for a quick clean-up after a walk on the beach.

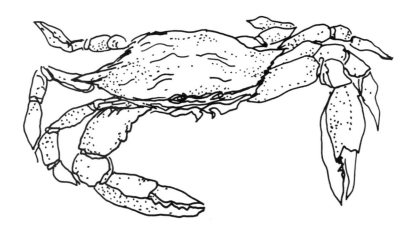

TYBEE LIGHTHOUSE/TYBEE MUSEUM

Tybee Island Historical Association
30 Meddin Drive
P.O. Box 366
Tybee Island, GA 31328
(912) 786-5801

∎∎∎∎∎∎∎∎∎∎∎∎∎∎∎∎∎∎∎∎∎∎∎∎∎∎∎∎∎∎

DAYS/HOURS OF OPERATION
10 AM - 6 PM daily
Closed Tuesdays

ADMISSION
$2.50 per adult
$.75 per child, 6-12
Children under 6, free
$1.50 per senior citizen

FACILITIES
Drink machine
Gift Shop
Parking
Restrooms
Visitor's Center

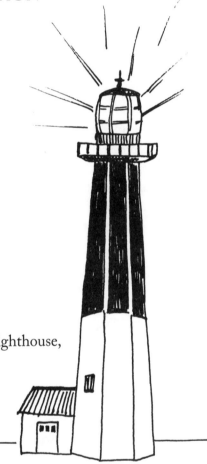

SPECIAL EVENTS
Candle Lantern Tour of Tybee Lighthouse,
  8 PM, Summer
$3 per adult
$2 per child

HINTS
* Sunscreen
* Cool drinks, during summer
* Allow two hours

"My favorite thing about this visit was the little pirate guns at the museum and the model of the circle! I liked going to the top of the lighthouse and looking at the ocean and going up the stairs and counting them."
Billy McKee, age 4

Going to the beach is usually appealing to children of all ages. With the additional attraction of a lighthouse and a museum in an old fort, enthusiasm doubles. Located on the northern tip of Tybee Island, the lighthouse was first established in 1736, just three years after James Oglethorpe settled on the Savannah River. Although the lighthouse standing today is not the original, the bottom sixty feet were constructed in 1773, and the upper ninety-four feet date to 1867. A beacon, the original Fresnal lens from 1867, shines at the top of the lighthouse, which can be seen eighteen miles away.

Children and energetic adults will enjoy the 178-step climb to the top of the tower. The view from the top of the lighthouse on a clear day stretches for miles in all directions, although it takes a stout-hearted person to stand for long on the narrow metal ledge which encircles the top.

Lighthouses carry an aura of historical romance about them. The Tybee light is no exception. It has seen two major wars—The Revolutionary War and the Civil War— and countless storms and hurricanes. Yet, the Tybee light continues to shine, greeting Savannah port visitors as they enter the mouth of the Savannah River. The lighthouse anchors a five-acre site with a cluster of six historical buildings which include the lighthouse keeper's cottage, a separate kitchen, an oil house, the first assistant keeper's cottage, and a soldier's barracks from the Civil War.

The lighthouse is maintained by the Tybee Island Historical Society through a lease arrangement with the U.S. Coast Guard.

Across the street from the lighthouse is the **Tybee Museum**. Located in part of Old Fort Screven, built in 1897, the museum's drab stucco exterior was designed to merge with the sandy beach landscape. At one time the batteries were covered to look like a sand dune in the effort to camouflage the fort.

Battery Garland houses the museum, and the network of small rooms and narrow stairways, halls and small angular windows will fulfill a child's desire to explore and discover. Numerous varied exhibits fill the museum. One details the history of Fort Screven, another the construction of the Martello Tower on Tybee which began in 1815. Panoramas, dioramas, paintings, Native American displays, shell exhibits, historic diving equipment, and historical artifacts fill the maze of rooms. Visitors will end at a narrow stairway which leads to the roof. Although railings are present, it is best to keep young children by the hand and in close view. The observation deck on the roof provides a great view of the Savannah River entrance and the Atlantic Ocean.

Parking is plentiful with a boardwalk to the beach from the museum. Like the lighthouse, the museum is operated by the Tybee Island Historical Society, a non-profit organization.

MIDTOWN AND
SOUTHWEST SAVANNAH

1. The Bamboo Farm
2. Daffin Park
3. L. Scott Stell Park
4. The Savannah Science Museum

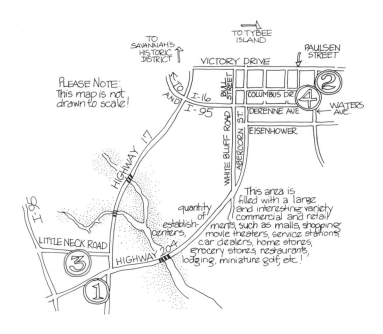

THE BAMBOO FARM

University of Georgia Cooperative Extension Service
2 Canebrake Road
Savannah, GA 31411
(912) 921-5461

DAYS/HOURS OF OPERATION
Daily, sunup to sundown

ADMISSION
Free

FACILITIES
Conference rooms
Greenhouse, flower beds
Parking
Picnic areas, including a pavilion that seats 288 people
Pets on leash
Restrooms
Trails

HINTS
* Picnic
* Bug Spray
* Allow one hour minimum

"I heard lots of bees buzzing and I watched out for
them. They were on the flowers. I liked walking
on the wood (flower bed borders)."
Katie Ratterree, age 3

Curiosity about the name may prompt a visit to the Bamboo
Farm, where bamboo is grown to feed panda bears in several major
U.S. and Canadian zoos. This site is not widely promoted, function-
ing primarily as a vegetative research center officially known as the
Coastal Area Extension Center of the University of Georgia Coop-

erative Extension Service. However, year-round visitors are common, and the superintendent reports a heavy turnout on Christmas Day.

The Bamboo Farm was established in 1919 by the U.S. Department of Agriculture for the introduction of Oriental and other non-native seeds and plants. New species of plants were studied and evaluated for their adaptability to the coastal climate, and bamboo is one of many plants which thrived here. Now operated by the Extension Service, the Bamboo Farm is most accurately described as a working botanical garden.

The Bamboo Farm doesn't look like a research center. The forty-six acre site resembles a rambling garden divided into sections and dotted with small home-like buildings, greenhouses, and occasional piles of cocoa shells and pine bark used as mulch. In the spring and summer beds of roses, 530 varieties of daylilies, dianthus, petunias, sunflowers, and many other annuals and perennials offer brilliant displays of color. Food crops are developed on a seasonal basis, and shrubs and trees are grown also. One favorite selection is hibiscus, and the Bamboo Farm tends over 200 varieties of this plant. A large herb section features a variety of scents, flowers, and textures, and attracts quantities of bees. Care should be taken with very young children. The greenhouses contain different plants in each growing season. Garden markers throughout the Bamboo Farm assist with plant identification. During periods of extreme heat and drought, sprinklers abound, and may come on unexpectedly.

This facility is clean and well-kept. There is a picnic area near one of the two lakes which is protected by an open-air pavilion with a 30' x 30' deck over the water. Bamboo has been put to use everywhere: as a decorative treatment for trash containers and planter boxes, as well as for fencing, path borders, and trellises. Parking is free, and there are spaces designated for handicapped parking. Paths through the various garden sections are not paved, but there are no obstacles for wheelchairs.

The few staff people present are quite busy, and generally not available for tours or extensive information, except for organized groups such as school groups and garden clubs. A visit to the Bamboo Farm will be more enjoyable for young children (ages 3 - 8) if there is a plan: a picnic, crayons and paper for drawing and coloring flowers and trees, a species hunt, or a color search.

DAFFIN PARK

1301 East Victory Drive
Savannah, GA 31405
(912) 351-3837

DAYS/HOURS OF OPERATION
Sunup to 9 PM

ADMISSION
Free for park; Hourly fees for tennis courts; Rental fee for pavilion
use or exclusive use of any park area

FACILITIES
Baseball diamonds
Basketball court
Fishing
Football fields
Handicapped access
Parking
Pets on leash
Picnic area
Playground
Pond
Restrooms (accessible for handicapped)
Shelter
Swimming pool
Soccer fields
Stadium
Tennis courts
Track (1.5 miles)

HINTS
* Great place for birthday parties
* Bug spray during spring and fall
* Baseball season provides opportunities for stadium parties; call
  351-9150 for more information on special baseball parties

"You can see fish swimming in the pond. In the pavilion you feel like you are on an island."
Katie Ratterree, age 4

In a city which clearly loves parks, Daffin Park is one of the most diverse. Few parks in any city can claim Daffin's combination of natural beauty and a wide variety of recreational amenities. Its central location along palm-lined Victory Drive makes this park accessible to many neighborhoods.

The 77-acre park was begun in 1908. The original plan, drawn by a landscape professional, has adapted well over the years to the community's growing recreational needs. The park is named for P. D. Daffin, who was Chairman of the Park and Tree Commission for 31 years, until his death in 1929.

Avenues of live oak trees define the park space and provide shade to drives and walkways. The center of the park is encircled by a drive and flanked by tennis courts, a swimming pool, and playing fields used for rugby, soccer, baseball, softball, and football. The western end of Daffin features an attractive, fenced playground that is accessible for the physically handicapped and wheelchairs. Along Victory Drive, there is a large pond with a covered pavilion in its center. The most prominent features of the pond are its two fountains, which shoot enormous sprays of water into the air. In recent years, the Rotary Club of Savannah has adopted the pond as a project and has been responsible for enhancing its beauty with the fountains, sidewalks, and lighting. The pond is also stocked with fish.

The eastern section of the park consists mainly of Grayson Stadium. This structure was built in the 1940s on the site of an earlier, wooden stadium that was destroyed in a major hurricane in August, 1940. Today, Grayson Stadium is home to the Savannah Cardinals, a minor league farm team of the St. Louis Cardinals. Near the stadium are picnic areas within a grove of pine trees. A jogging path of 1.5 miles encircles the entire park.

Mornings at Daffin find walkers, joggers, and pre-schoolers. Afternoons, the playing fields come to life with team sports. The tennis courts are popular year-round, all day long. Youth-league sports and home games of the Cardinals bring the park to life at night. For all ages, Daffin Park is one of Savannah's most popular destinations.

L. SCOTT STELL COMMUNITY PARK

Managed by Chatham County Department of Parks,
    Recreation and Cultural Affairs
P.O. Box 1746
Savannah, GA 31402
(912) 925-8694 / 921-0039
Location: 383 Bush Road

DAYS/HOURS OF OPERATION
Spring, Summer 8 AM to 11 PM
Fall, Winter 8 AM to 10 PM

ADMISSION
Free

FACILITIES
Bike trail
Camping (through special arrangements)
Handicapped access
Office
Parking
Picnic areas
Restrooms
Shelters
Snack Bar during sports games
Sports fields and courts

SPECIAL EVENTS
Summer Camps, June through August

HINTS
* Bring a picnic or snack
* Bring dirt bikes!
* Bring some bait for fishing
* Might want lawn chairs

"We liked seeing the ducks on the lake and we wanted our bikes for the bike trail!"

Tom McKee, age 10
Tony Zabarac, age 10

Chatham County's L. Scott Stell Community Park, tucked away between Highway 204 and Littleneck Road, is a gem of a park. Spread out over 108 acres, this park formerly served the federal government as a helicopter training field during the Vietnam War. The roads in the park are the old runways, and park officials continue to refer to them as runways. Landing markers and painted lines from practice days are still visible. Even the tennis courts are built on a section of the old runway. Called the Ogeechee Stage Field, this land was transferred to Chatham County from the federal government for $1.00.

Children will enjoy feeding or watching the ducks which swim on the man-made S-shaped lake. Surrounding the lake is a one-mile jogging/hiking trail for exercising or a casual stroll. For children who may want to try their luck fishing, the park will provide poles, fishing line, and hooks. All would-be fishermen need is bait. Fishing is free, and the lake is stocked with bass, crappie, catfish, and bream!

There is a playground near two large picnic areas with a few covered pavilions. A bike hill and short dirt bike trail may capture the interest of young bikers with plenty of additional space to ride.

Possibly one of the most unique features of this park is the opportunity to plant one's own garden in one of 93 free garden spots located around the perimeter of one of the "runways." Park personnel see that the soil is plowed and prepared for planting. All they ask of gardeners is to plant, maintain, and harvest their crops. A huge pile of compost is located to the side of the garden plots. This is a great opportunity for children to have first-hand experience with growing their own vegetables.

Practicing baseball, soccer, tennis, and volleyball are on-going, and traffic in the park may vary according to scheduled games. There seems to be ample parking for all with lots of wide open spaces for running around, flying a kite, playing ball, and just plain having fun!

THE SAVANNAH SCIENCE MUSEUM

4405 Paulsen Street
Savannah, GA 31405
(912) 355-6705

- -

DAYS/HOURS OF OPERATION
Tuesday-Saturday, 10 AM to 5 PM
Sunday, 2 PM to 5 PM
Closed Mondays and holidays

ADMISSION
Members free
$3 per adult
$2 per child under 12
$2 per person group rate
Children 3 and under are free

FACILITIES
Food/Drink vending machines
Gift shop
Handicapped access
Parking
Restrooms
Recycling bins for newspaper, magazines, office paper, and
   aluminum cans only.

SPECIAL EVENTS
Planetarium shows for school groups, Monday through Friday
Planetarium shows for general public, Second Sundays, 3 PM
Traveling exhibits
Lectures
Summer camps
Children's programs
Group tours
Shows
The Caretta Research Project (summer turtling on Wassaw Island.)

HINTS
* Allow two hours for visit, if attending a program
* Call ahead for hours of special programs
* Birthday parties encouraged! Reservations required with advance arrangements for special programs.

"I liked the snakes and reptiles show the best!"
Margaret Spence, age 10

Whales! Turtles! Rocks and minerals! Fossils! Stars and planets! A giant ground sloth skeleton! All museums hold the promise or learning, and the Savannah Science Museum is no exception.

Tucked away at 60th and Paulsen Streets, the Savannah Science Museum has recently expanded to include a 150-seat auditorium and a Foucault Pendulum in a glass tower which can be seen from the street. In harmony with the rotation of the earth, the pendulum knocks down one wooden peg after the other that are positioned in a circle.

Exhibits of fossils are arranged in the main lobby under the banner, "Prehistoric Creatures From Your Backyard." Several glass cases

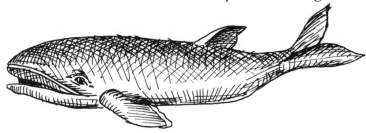

display an impressive array of prehistoric Indian spearpoints, arrowheads, and tools representative of the cultural periods.

Planetarium shows are given regularly during the day by a full-time planetarium director. The wonder of the heavens will captivate visitors of all ages.

A newly-opened Discovery Room encourages hands-on participation from children of all ages. A living bee-hive, a zoetrope showing the first moving picture technology, trays of fossils, live turtles, and a plasma ball are just a few of the hands-on experiences awaiting visitors.

The auditorium off the main lobby is frequently in use. Snakes and reptiles, puppets, and Mr. Wizard Science Shows make regular appearances, as well as special lectures and unusual programs.

Although residents of Savannah know of the museum's collection of live snakes and reptiles, probably few realize that this museum houses one of the largest non-academic reptile and amphibian collections in the Southeast. Rattlesnakes, copperheads, rat snakes, king snakes, boa constrictors, and pythons are among the living residents in the Science Museum.

Several very special reptilian residents are loggerhead sea turtles which are part of a new exhibit, "Endangered Giants of the Georgia Coast: Whales and Turtles." Visitors step aboard the *S.S. Caretta*, a research vessel, which provides the rare opportunity of a close-up view of a young loggerhead sea turtle.

The Savannah Science Museum has been involved in protecting loggerhead sea turtles since 1971 through its Caretta Research Project. Participants from all over the United States pay their expenses to spend a week on uninhabited Wassaw Island, tagging and monitoring the female loggerheads who lumber up on to the beach to lay their eggs in the dunes during the summer months. This project, a joint effort with the U.S. Fish & Wildlife Service and the Wassaw Trust, is not only one of the most popular educational programs at the Science Museum, but also is one of the longest running projects of its type in the United States.

The other half of this exhibit centers around the 15-foot skeleton of a baby northern right whale, which is displayed in the manner in which it was found---half buried in the sand of a small barrier island (Little St. Simons) off Georgia's coast. Tucked away in a drawer for years, this skeleton has finally been preserved and assembled.

Other permanent exhibits include a well-labeled rocks and minerals display, shell identification, and a huge shadow box to challenge the most active child to stand still and create an unusual shadow. Traveling exhibits make frequent appearances, enticing visitors and school children to return again and again.

SOUTHEAST SAVANNAH AND ISLANDS

1. The Aquarium at Skidaway Island
2. Bethesda Home for Boys
3. Chatham County Garden Center and Botanical Gardens
4. Lake Mayer
5. Skidaway Island State Park
6. Wormsloe Historic Site

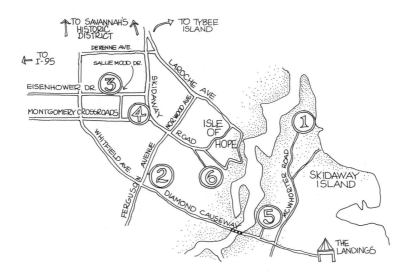

THE AQUARIUM AT SKIDAWAY ISLAND

University of Georgia Marine Extension Service
30 Ocean Science Circle
Savannah, GA 31411
(912) 598-2496

DAYS/HOURS OF OPERATION
Monday - Friday, 9 AM to 4 PM
Saturday, Noon to 5 PM

ADMISSION
$1 per person; Children under 6, free

FACILITIES
Gift Shop
Parking
Picnic area
Recycling bins
Restrooms
Trails
Vending machines

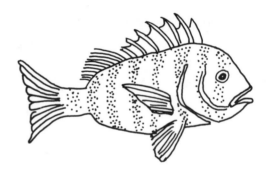

SPECIAL EVENTS
Sea Camp for children ages 8 to 14, with weekly sessions
  in July and August

HINTS
* Take a picnic
* Bug spray
* Allow one hour for the Aquarium; add one hour for trail
  and picnic

**"I liked looking at the sharks most. I also like the nature
trail. We've seen deer on the trail before."**
Joe Ratterree, age 8

The Aquarium at Skidaway Island is a favorite outing for all ages. Its beautiful setting overlooking the Skidaway River is reason enough to make this a destination, but the Aquarium offers more than scenery. The Aquarium is part of a large complex which includes The University of Georgia Marine Extension Service and the Skidaway Institute of Oceanography. While some of the facilities are reserved for research and conference purposes, the Aquarium, picnic area, and nature trail are open to the public.

The Aquarium focuses on Georgia's marine and estuarine animals with regional fish of all shapes, sizes and colors. The main exhibit space, sensibly laid out and easy to follow, consists of wall tanks housing various species of fish and invertebrates. Labels are easy to read and well illustrated. Step-up platforms and handrails allow face-to-face encounters with fish, sharks, and turtles. Other exhibits at the Aquarium display historical and prehistorical uses of coastal resources, shells, skulls, and other artifacts. On Saturdays, an informative video is shown, and photography and art exhibits with environmental themes are presented on a seasonal schedule. A favorite activity is to take crayons or markers, and draw pictures of the fish and their habitats.

It is wise to plan enough time for enjoying the Jay Wolf nature trail. Approximately one mile in length, the path takes in coastal vistas as well as woodlands. Selected native trees are clearly marked. At low tide, children enjoy walking along the marsh's edge and chasing the elusive fiddler crab, while a shaded bench overlooking the marsh and river is a tempting resting spot for grown-ups. Along the wooded part of the trail, it is not unusual to hear the footsteps of deer, and more often than not they will make a fleeting appearance.

The picnic area is located between the Aquarium and the entrance to the nature trail. Shady, cool, and offering magnificent views of the Skidaway River, this spot calls for an outing planned around meal or snack time, or even a party. Group gatherings are welcome with food limited to the picnic area.

Staff at the Aquarium are predominantly behind-the-scenes, but can be summoned from the office to answer questions or offer other assistance. A small shop within the office offers t-shirts, local maps and booklets, and post cards.

BETHESDA HOME FOR BOYS

Union Society of Savannah
P.O. Box 13039
Savannah, GA 31499
(912) 351-2040
Located at 9520 Ferguson Ave.

▪ ▪

DAYS/HOURS OF OPERATION
Museum and Office Hours, Monday - Friday, 9 AM - 5 PM
Nature trail and chapel, sunrise to sunset

ADMISSION
Free; donations accepted

FACILITIES
Parking
Picnic area
Restrooms
Trail
Water fountain

SPECIAL EVENTS
Annual Labor Day festival with arts and crafts, games and rides,
food, silent auction, entertainment. Parking fee.

HINTS
* Bug Spray
* Allow 1 hour
* Bring a picnic

"My favorite part of the visit was seeing the raccoon
climb up and go into the dead Palmetto tree."
Joe Ratterree, age 10
Tom McKee, Jr., age 10

"My favorite part of the visit was seeing the pecan trees and finding some pecans." (October)

Billy McKee, age 5

Listed on the National Register of Historic Places, a visit to Bethesda is a step back into a graceful era uncluttered by the noise of traffic. A traditional brick archway, constructed in 1938, marks the entrance to Bethesda. Visitors then drive down a majestic live-oak-lined lane to a cluster of historic and modern buildings which comprise the Bethesda Boys Home.

Bethesda's peaceful, pastoral setting on the banks of the Moon River (made famous by Johnny Mercer's song of the same name) is directly opposite historic Wormsloe Plantation. The view from Bethesda today is similar to the same view two hundred years before.

Founded in 1740 by George Whitefield and James Habersham, as an orphanage, Bethesda was located on a King's Grant of land (500 acres) by the Royal Charter of 1732. The orphanage was relatively self-sufficient, raising its own food through a productive garden and tending livestock. Today, pastures of grazing cows and horses can be seen from Ferguson Avenue or from the nature trail, continuing the tradition begun in 1740.

In 1801, after the establishment of the Savannah Home for Girls, Bethesda limited its residents to boys. Bethesda is managed by the Union Society, a benevolent society established in 1750.

The museum is located in the Burroughs Cottage (1883), Bethesda's oldest remaining building. A tabby brick walk leads the visitor to the Cunningham Historic Center (the museum) which is filled with portraits; pictures; a model of Bethesda; reading tables; eclectic collections of bones, rocks, tools, bottles; and models of ships.

The Whitefield Chapel, located next to Burrough's Cottage, was constructed in 1925 in memory of the founder of Bethesda. Children may want to notice the brick floors in the herringbone pattern, stained glass windows, and moveable wooden pews. A visit to the balcony provides a bird's eye view of both Bethesda and the chapel.

The 1/2 mile nature trail, opened in May, 1993, begins just behind the office at the base of a magnificent live oak tree. A map with
detailed marker-by-marker descriptions is located in a large black
mailbox at the start of the trail. Wooden markers along the trail identify primarily trees, as well as scenic vistas and historic sites. Spectacu-
lar marsh views, ancient live oaks, and rural pasture are hallmarks of
the trail, which is well worth the hike even with young children. There
is even a dock on a creek which at high tide holds promise for crab-
bing, shrimping, and fishing. It would be wise first to seek permission
from the office, however, before throwing in a line.

Over the two centuries of Bethesda's existence, more than 8000
children have lived at Bethesda. Currently, Bethesda operates a resi-
dential facility for boys who need a more structured environment.
Programs for the boys at Bethesda allow for growth in the academic,
spiritual, and physical areas. An on-campus school was opened in
September, 1992 for grades three through eight. Future years will see
the expansion of these grades. Bethesda means "House of Mercy," and
it continues to carry on its mission of mercy even after 254 years.

CHATHAM COUNTY GARDEN CENTER AND BOTANICAL GARDENS

Managed by the Savannah Area Council of Garden Clubs, Inc.
1388 Eisenhower Drive
Savannah, GA 31406
(912) 355-3883

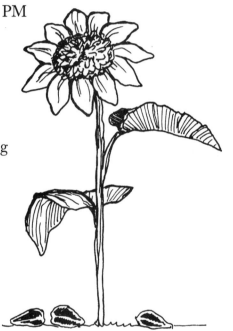

DAYS/HOURS OF OPERATION
Monday through Friday, 10 AM to 2 PM

ADMISSION
Donations accepted

FACILITIES
Garden paths
Handicapped access in rear of building
Parking
Restroom
Trails
Visitors center

SPECIAL EVENTS
Classes held on gardening subjects
Plant sales
Group Tours

"It's neat that they are arranging things so that there will always be something in bloom when you go."
Mary Ellen McKee, age 13

For a refreshing escape from the hustle and bustle of day-to-day routine, a visit to the Garden Center and Botanical Gardens will be well worth the time. With fall, winter, spring, and summer gardens planned, there will always be something blooming.

Each of Savannah's garden club has its own plot of garden to cultivate, producing a broad variety of gardens on the 10-acre site. The range of planned gardens includes an herb garden, vegetable garden, perennial garden, rose garden, scent garden, courtyard garden, native plant garden, and a shade garden. Two graceful gazebos with inviting benches underneath will have planted arbors. A garden for children is also planned.

The Garden Center and Botanical Gardens is one of the newest sites in Chatham County. The land for the gardens was donated by Chatham County. The restored 1840's farmhouse located on the site was originally located at Rinehardt Plantation. The farmhouse was moved to Helmken Street to make way for a cemetery, then had to be moved again to make way for the Truman Parkway. Garden Club members have painstakingly restored the house to its original condition and furnished the downstairs parlor, dining room, and hall with period furniture. Upstairs are Garden Club Council offices and a classroom where classes on flower arranging, landscape design, pruning, tree planting, and other garden related activities will be held.

The site contains a wetland area which will be enhanced, and nature trails into a forested area are also planned. Trees will be identified by markers along the trail when the trail is completed. Garden classes for children will occasionally be offered which will make this site unique in Savannah.

LAKE MAYER PARK

Montgomery Crossroads at Sallie Mood Drive
Savannah, GA 31406
(912) 652-6780
(912) 652-6786

- -

DAYS/HOURS OF OPERATION
8 AM to 10 PM, Fall/Winter
8 AM to 11 PM, Spring/Summer

ADMISSION
Free

FACILITIES
Basketball courts (2)
Boat rental, ramp and dock
Fishing
Handball court
Handicapped access
Parking
Picnic areas (open and covered)
Playground
Restrooms and shower
Shelter
Tennis courts (8)
Track (1.5 miles)
Vending machines

HINTS
* Take a picnic
* Bug Spray recommended in spring and fall months
* Good place for beginner fishing
* Take stale bread to feed ducks and geese
* Fun place for birthday parties! Pavilions available for rent.

"When I was 3, my dad brought me here and taught me how to fish."
Joe Ratterree, age 9

"I like to feed bread to the ducks."
Katie Ratterree, age 5

Lake Mayer is a 75-acre community park with enough recreational activities to keep most people busy for hours. It is named for the late Henry Mayer, the Chatham County Commissioner who in the 1950's conceived the idea for this park. Completed in 1972, Lake Mayer Park is encircled by a 35-acre lake which is stocked with bass, bream, channel catfish, and more. This park is popular year-round, and during the spring and fall months it bustles with people and activities.

If there is any one place in Chatham County where the entire family can have a good time, this is it. Mom and Dad can jog or walk the 1.5 mile track while younger ones bike or skate alongside. There are 8 tennis courts, 2 basketball courts, a handball court, and a playground. Fishing is permitted just about anywhere on the lake, but the area near the picnic tables is a favorite spot for beginners who are almost guaranteed a nibble by some of the little fish. A small can of whole kernel corn will provide more than enough bait for a morning or afternoon of casting.

One of the favorite activities for Lake Mayer visitors is feeding the ducks and geese who live within the park. When the park opened, 15 baby ducklings were introduced. Over the years, especially just after Easter, other ducklings have come to live here, and the population has grown to include mallards and wood ducks. There are also geese and seagulls in huge flocks. During the early spring months ducks and geese are nesting, and a few weeks later flocks of babies waddle around after their mothers. Whatever the variety or size of winged animal, they are all hungry and enjoy eating bread crumbs and crackers. A mild word of caution - hungry geese can be rather aggressive, and some are actually taller than small toddlers.

Classes in boating, sailing, karate, arts and crafts, and other activities are available during the year. There are several annual festivals and events held here, also. The pavilions can be rented for private use.

SKIDAWAY ISLAND STATE PARK

Managed by The Georgia Department of Natural Resources
52 Diamond Causeway
Skidaway Island
Savannah, Georgia 31406
(912) 598-2300, 598-2301

DAYS/HOURS OF OPERATION
7 AM until 10 PM, daily
Park office hours, 8 AM until 5 PM
(Open until 10 PM during the summer)

ADMISSION
$2 per car

FACILITIES
Camping
Food/drink machines
Handicapped access
Parking
Pets on leash
Phones
Picnic areas
Restrooms
Shelters
Snack Bar, Memorial Day to Labor Day
Swimming pool, Memorial Day to Labor Day
Trails
Visitors Center

SPECIAL EVENTS
Coastal Birds Program (April)
Seafood Delights (Fall)
Wild Game Cooking (Winter)

HINTS

* For fall, spring, or summer visits, bring bug spray
* Bring a picnic lunch, particularly drinks
* Good place for bike riding
* Bring stroller or baby carrier for young children
* Allow 2 to 3 hours
* Bring binoculars
* Guided hikes available with advance reservations
* Shelters can be reserved for parties. Playgrounds, trails, camp ground, and lots of picnic tables foster many party possibilities.

"My favorite part was the playground, particularly the tire swing."
Tom McKee, Jr. age 10

"I liked walking on the trails."
Jessica Konter, age 12

"I liked seeing the wildlife and the marsh."
Mary Ellen McKee, age 13

Skidaway Island State Park encompasses 533 acres including large expanses of salt marsh, freshwater wetlands, and mixed pine/hardwood forest. This is the only state park in Chatham County with camping facilities (88 tent and trailer sites), plus it boasts a Junior Olympic Swimming Pool, 5 large picnic areas with shelters, playgrounds, and an amphitheatre.

The park, located on the inland edge of Skidaway Island, is accessible by car. Of historic interest, the park contains two large Confederate earthworks which were built to protect Skidaway Narrows.

There are two trails within the park and guided trail hikes are available with advance reservations. Maps of the park and the two trails are available at the park office. The Big Ferry Nature Trail is three miles long and takes approximately an hour and a half to hike at a relaxed pace. Winding through the woods, over wetlands, and skirting the salt marsh this trail has side trips to an old moonshine still and the Confederate earth works. Educational markers along the trail point out natural, archeological, and historical highlights.

There is an Indian shell midden from the late Archaic period which shows human activity from two thousand years ago. Even the Indians liked to eat oysters!

The other trail, the Sandpiper Trail, begins behind the visitor's center. It is a mile long and takes approximately twenty minutes to hike. The trail guide coordinates trail markers with questions and answers along the way, and visitors on this trail have one of the best opportunities to observe the salt marsh up-close. Fiddler crabs scurry away in huge armies as children approach. Depending on the season, a marsh hawk, osprey, or red-tailed hawk may be spotted. The impressionable marsh mud always holds tracks of raccoons, deer, or wading birds. A look-out tower, a favorite with children, provides a birds-eye view of the large expanse of marsh.

There is plenty to do here for a day-long family outing, a church picnic, or a school field trip. Advance reservations for groups are recommended because Skidaway Island State Park is a popular destination for many.

WORMSLOE HISTORIC SITE

7601 Skidaway Road
Savannah, GA 31406
(912) 353-3023

■■■

DAYS/HOURS OF OPERATION
Tuesday - Saturday, 9 AM to 5 PM
Sunday, 2 PM to 5 PM
Closed Monday, except legal holidays
Closed Thanksgiving, Christmas, and New Year's Day

ADMISSION
$2 per adult
$1 per child under 18
$1.50 per adult for tour groups (15 or more)
$.50 per person for youth groups (15 or more)
(Bus drivers and group leaders free)

FACILITIES
Audio-visual presentation
Brochures
Drink machines
Handicapped access in museum; wheelchair access in museum and
   along wide trail; wheelchair available on site; prior arrangements
   can be made for vehicular transport of handicapped people.
Gift shop
Picnic area
Museum
Parking
Restrooms

HINTS
* Allow 1 hour minimum
* Great place for children to run around
* Bug spray advisable in warm seasons
* Advance reservations required for large groups

"I like the trails through the woods. We went here with my cub scouts. This is a great place to go with friends."
Joe Ratterree, age 9

One of the most breathtaking vistas in the Low Country is the one and a half mile drive into Wormsloe under the magnificent canopy of live oaks. These trees were planted in 1892-1893 to honor the birth of a descendant of Wormsloe's original owner, Noble Jones. The gates at the entrance of the drive were added when this same descendant turned 21.

In 1736, three years after the colony of Georgia was established at Savannah, founder James Edward Oglethorpe dispatched fellow colonist Noble Jones to a site south of town near a bend in the Skidaway River. Jones' mission was to build a fortified colonial outpost to protect the new settlement from attack by the Spanish in Florida.

Fortunately, the colonists never encountered the Spanish in local waters. The over 800 acres of land known as Wormsloe (the name possibly derived from a Welsh name meaning "dragon's lair") remained in the hands of Jones' descendants until 1973, when most of the property was sold to the State of Georgia via The Nature Conservancy to be operated as a historic site. All that remains of the fortified house built by Jones and his men is the tabby foundation of the house and much of the surrounding walls, but a beautifully made, scale model of the house is on display for visitors.

The first stop after the parking lot is the museum where the offices, small auditorium, and a gallery of exhibits are located. Restrooms and a vending machine are reached through a different entrance. A seventeen-minute audio visual overview of the site is shown frequently and highly recommended. Following that, visitors enter the exhibit area through iron gates designed for the museum by well-known ironsmith Ivan Bailey. Well-labeled wall maps, artifact displays, and scale models of Jones' house, Fort Frederica, a Spanish fort, and an Indian village all assist in interpreting the coastal fortification system of colonial days. Site rangers are available to answer questions.

After leaving the museum building there are two paths from which to choose, each ending at the site of Mr. Jones' first house. The wide path is the most direct, but the interpretive nature trail, slightly longer, is more intriguing. The latter wanders through the woods and around beautiful views of the marsh and river through moss-laden trees. Just off the path is a clearing featuring a small wooden structure and a corral. This area is used for living history demonstrations for groups and special occasions. The small house is an example of wattle and daub (or in 20th century words, mud and sticks) construction. Every effort should be made to visit Wormsloe during one of these demonstrations when people dress in colonial garb and act out a day in the life of colonial Georgia.

The path eventually opens onto a cleared area revealing the tabby foundation and surrounding walls of Mr. Jones' house. Tabby, a mixture of sand, oyster shell and lime, was the colonial equivalent of cement, and suitable for structures built near the water. The tabby foundation and walls here are one of the oldest remaining structures from Oglethorpe's time in coastal Georgia period. A little imagination and common sense will assist children in figuring out the basic floor plan of this early Georgia home.

After passing the tabby ruins, explorers will come to a gravestone which was placed to commemorate the family of Noble Jones who are buried on the site. Both the wide trail and the interpretive nature trail lead back toward the museum and parking area.

FOR CHILDREN OVER 12

(ALL LOCATED IN HISTORIC DISTRICT)

1. Andrew Low House
2. Flannery O'Connor House
3. Green Meldrim House
4. Isaiah Davenport House
5. Owens-Thomas House

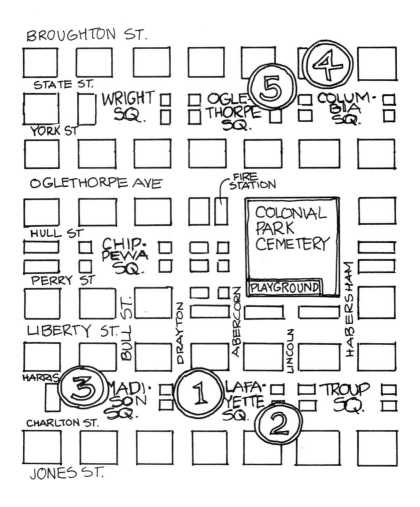

ANDREW LOW HOUSE

Headquarters of The National Society of
  The Colonial Dames of America
329 Abercorn Street
Savannah, GA 31401
(912) 233-6854

■ ■

DAYS/HOURS OF OPERATION
Weekdays, 10:30 AM to 4 PM
Sundays, Noon to 4 PM
Closed Thursdays, National Holidays, and December 13-27

ADMISSION
$5 per person
$2 students under 18
$1 children under 12 and Girl Scouts
Tour Groups $2 per person

"The old glass bookcase panes were fascinating. To think of glass as a liquid just baffles me!
Thomas Beason, age 12

    The sophisticated Andrew Low House, circa 1848, combines European elegance with West Indian plantation influence. Andrew Low's famous daughter-in-law, Juliette Gordon Low, lived here from 1886 until 1927. For Girl Scouts everywhere, this house deserves a pilgrimage. In the morning room in the front of the house, Juliette Gordon Low signed the original charter to found the Girl Scouts in 1912. It was also in an upstairs bedroom that the founder of the Girl Scouts died in 1927.

    Facing Lafayette Square, the house was designed by architect John Norris of New York for the wealthy cotton merchant, Andrew Low. Andrew Low came from Scotland to Savannah to become a cotton exporter, but he maintained a baronial castle in England and only spent his winters in Savannah. It was Andrew's son, William, who married Juliette Gordon Low.

Is glass a liquid or a solid? Surprisingly enough, it is a liquid! Children will be interested to see old glass panes in the bookcase of the morning room which are slowly dripping downward, thinning at the top. The house is furnished in period antiques and during the time of Andrew Low there were over fifteen servants managing this household.

Two historic figures were guests in this house. Southern General Robert E. Lee stayed here in 1870, and he had the honor of being named the godfather of Andrew Low's youngest daughter. Also, William Makepeace Thackeray, author of *Vanity Fair*, stayed here in 1853 and 1856 when he was on lecture tours in the United States.

The formal dining room is grandly furnished and hails from another era when the children dined downstairs in the children's dining room. Children were not allowed to dine with the adults until they learned proper etiquette!

Another point of interest is the dry moat which surrounds the house outside. This dry moat followed a European design and was used as a passageway for the servants navigating outside the house.

Majestic, but frowning lions grace the entryway to the house. The expressions on the lions' faces denote pussycats rather than fierce lions, and it is said that Juliette Gordon Low patted the lions on the head as she entered and left the house.

The Colonial Dames of America maintain the house in keeping with its noble past. It is well worth a visit, and older children and girl scouts will enjoy this glimpse into sophisticated 19th century life. Well-informed guides provide entertaining, anecdotal, and historic information.

FLANNERY O'CONNOR HOUSE

Owned and Managed by The Flannery O'Connor Home
  Foundation, Inc.
207 East Charlton Street
Savannah, GA 31401
(912) 233-6014

■ ■

DAYS/HOURS OF OPERATION
Friday, Saturday, Sunday
1 PM to 4 PM

ADMISSION
Donations Accepted

SPECIAL EVENTS
Special Sunday programs, such as readings, guest lecturers, films,
  or seminars.

"This house is recommended for someone who has read
her work and knows who she is."
Mary Ellen McKee, age 13

Located on quiet Lafayette Square, the childhood home of
Southern novelist Flannery O'Connor is a modest four-story stucco
house. A historical marker is located in front of the house with a brief
history of Flannery O'Connor who died in 1964 at the early age of 39.

Flannery O'Connor spent the first thirteen years of her life here
in this house and around Lafayette Square. She attended the Cathedral and Catholic school on the square, and the faith and symbols of
Catholicism play an important role in her short stories and novels.

The house was purchased in 1989 by the O'Connor Home Foundation, and currently only the parlor floor and a courtyard garden,
recently designed and planted, are open to the public. Plans by the
Foundation include further restoration and utilizing the house as a
literary center for Savannah with the particular focus on Southern
literature.

Flannery O'Connor stands beside William Faulkner, Eudora Welty, and Walker Percy as a distinguished Southern writer. She won the O'Henry Award for the best short story of the year on three separate occasions and a collection of her short stories won the National Book Award in 1972. As a child in the O'Connor home, she helped raise ducks and chickens in the courtyard and even taught a chicken to walk backwards. Notecards bearing the design of the house are sold inside.

GREEN-MELDRIM HOUSE

14 West Macon Street
On Madison Square
Savannah, GA 31401
(912) 233-3845

- -

DAYS/HOURS OF OPERATION
Tuesday, Thursday,Friday, Saturday, 10 AM to 4 PM
Closed December 15 through January 15 and
  two weeks prior to Easter

ADMISSION
$3 per person

FACILITIES
Restrooms

HINTS
* Combine with a Madison Square outing

The Green-Meldrim House was completed in 1853 as the residence of Charles Green. This Gothic revival-style house was designed by John Norris, a New York architect who also designed Massie School, the United States Custom House, and the Andrew Low Mansion. In 1892 the house was bought by Judge Peter Meldrim, and in 1943 St. John's Episcopal Church purchased it for use as a parish house.

In addition to its architectural and historical significance, the Green-Meldrim House is well known as the house used by Union General William Tecumseh Sherman as headquarters in 1864, at the end of his march to the sea. Owner Charles Green gave up most of the house to the general and his troops. Shortly after moving in, General Sherman sent a telegram to Abraham Lincoln, offering the city of Savannah to him as a Christmas present. Charles Green's hospitality may have prevented Savannah from the total destruction that Sherman inflicted upon other southern towns along his route.

The grandeur of this house is evident from the moment visitors approach. Entry to the house is through three sets of doors. The massive outer doors, almost intimidating, are compatible with the gothic style of the house. Inside, the rooms are spacious and cool, with high ceilings and tiled floors. Much of the interior door hardware is silver-plated. Elaborate crown moldings, marble mantles, and enormous chandeliers reflect the elegance of the home.

Visitors will enjoy a guided tour which takes between 30 and 40 minutes. Docents will point out furnishings and other details significant to the history of the house. After touring the house, visitors will want to view the garden and wading pool.

ISAIAH DAVENPORT HOUSE MUSEUM

Owned and managed by Historic Savannah Foundation, Inc.
324 East State Street
Savannah, GA 31401
(912) 236-8097

■■

DAYS/HOURS OF OPERATION
Daily 10 AM to 4:30 PM
Closed Major Holidays

ADMISSION
$4 per adult
$3 per child (6 to 18 years)
Five and under Free
Museum Shop and Garden, No charge

HINTS
*Tours are given on the hour and half hour
*Last tour at 4 PM

> **"A lot of old-timey details that you have to notice, like the plaster work or designs and the pictures on the wall, make this a neat house."**
> *Mary Ellen McKee, age 13*

Located on charming Columbia Square, the Davenport House is an elegant reminder of the past. Built in 1820, by Master Builder Isaiah Davenport, it is a classic example of federal architecture that survives today because of a gallant rescue attempt which succeeded and led to the formation of Historic Savannah Foundation, Inc.

During the 1930's, the Davenport House had been turned into apartments, dividing floors into separate apartments. In the 1950's, the four stories of this gracious house were destined for demolition. The space remaining was planned as a parking lot. Fortunately, seven courageous and energetic women raised the money necessary to purchase the house to save it from destruction, and Historic Savannah Foundation was formed. Today, many visitors may enjoy this architectural treasure.

The Davenport House's four floors are open for viewing plus the outdoor garden. The large gift shop carries many items unique to Savannah as well as reproductions that may have been used in Isaiah Davenport's time period, the early 19th century. Period furniture and furnishings decorate the house, and the architectural details in the rooms, on the stairways and doorways, and around the windows are what make the Davenport House worth a visit.

OWENS-THOMAS HOUSE

Owned by the Telfair Academy of Arts and Sciences
124 Abercorn Street
Savannah, GA 31401
(912) 233-9743

DAYS/HOURS OF OPERATION
Tuesday-Saturday, 10 AM to 5 PM
Sunday - Monday, 2 PM to 5 PM
(Last tour begins at 4:30)

ADMISSION
Members of Telfair free
$5 per adult
$3 students
$2 children 6 to 12

FACILITIES
Gift Shop

HINTS
* Allow 30 to 45 minutes

> "I've never seen such a big dining room table. A lot of
> people must have lived in this house."
> *Katie Ratterree, age 5*

> "It's neat to have a bridge inside a house!"
> *Joe Ratterree, age 10*

The Owens-Thomas House is one of America's finest examples of the Regency style of architecture. Like the Telfair Museum, it was designed by the English architect William Jay. This house was built in 1819 for cotton merchant and banker Richard Richardson and is a good representation of the house of a prominent, wealthy Savannahian at the time. Unfortunately, Mr. Richardson lived here only three years before bankruptcy. Afterwards, the house was run as a lodging house for several years. In 1825, the Revolutionary War hero, the Marquis de Lafayette, stayed here as a guest, and is said to have delivered a speech from the cast iron balcony overlooking President Street. The house was purchased by the Owens family in 1830. In 1951, an Owens descendant, Miss Margaret Thomas, left the house to the Telfair to be operated as a house museum.

From the moment visitors enter the front gates, it is evident that Mr. Jay, the architect, had a fondness for symmetry and for the forms and shapes found in ancient classical buildings. Columns, gentle curves and ellipses, and the Greek key design are some of the reminders of the classical tradition. After entering the house, visitors begin a docent-guided tour that takes about 30 minutes. Fidgety youngsters may prefer to chase butterflies in the garden (with Mom or Dad, of course) or toss pennies into the fountain.

The house is made of tabby, a mixture of lime, oyster shells and sand, and covered with stucco; an exposed area on the southern side of the house shows what the tabby looks like. Inside, there are unusual design features. The decorative corners of the drawing room make the ceiling appear rounded. In the dining room, there are curved walls and doors and an interestingly lit window with amber glass panes which gives the incoming light a soft glow.

The entry features a handpainted floorcloth, the 19th century version of linoleum and a practical floorcovering for houses on dusty streets. Upstairs, there is a bridge connecting two wings of the house. The balcony facing south is one of the earliest uses of cast iron in architecture in Savannah.

The garden is known as a *par terre* garden, referring to its symmetrical division into bordered beds. Children enjoy wandering its stone paths and throwing pennies into the center fountain.

The carriage house behind the garden has been the site of archaeological and historical research in preparation for its conversion into a visitors center in 1995 featuring an orientation gallery, museum shop, and restrooms.

ADDITIONAL INFORMATION

Readers are advised to call sites before visiting to confirm hours, days, admission fees, and to find out if there are special events taking place.

The Savannah Visitors Center (featured on page 40) is a good "first stop" for visitors.

The following index may be helpful in guiding readers to events and activities in addition to those occurring at the sites included in the book.

ARTS

Arts Line 233-2787
Savannah Symphony Society 236-9536
City Lights Theatre 234-9860
Coastal Jazz Association 232-2222
Savannah Leisure Services Bureau 351-3837
Savannah Theatre Company 233-7764
Lucas Theater for the Arts 232-1696
Art In the Park (Summer) 351-3837

RECREATION

Savannah Athletic Services 351-3852
Savannah Cardinals Baseball 351-9150
County Parks & Recreation 652-6780
Savannah Leisure Services Bureau 351-3837

FESTIVALS AND PARADES

Arts Line 233-2787
Savannah Waterfront Association 234-0295
Savannah Leisure Services Bureau 351-3837
County Parks & Recreation 652-6780
St. Patrick's Day Parade 233-4804

March 17 is St. Patrick's Day, and Savannah hosts one of the nation's largest parades. The downtown area is recommended that day only for those who wish to enjoy the parade, as many museums and sites in the area close on this day. Call first to be sure before making plans.

APPENDIX – LISTING OF SITES BY SUBJECT/THEME

ART

GARDENS

RESTAURANTS IN HISTORIC PLACES

HISTORIC SITES

MUSEUMS

NATURE TRAILS

PARKS AND PLAYGROUNDS

THE MEMORY GAME

FOR TWO OR MORE PLAYERS

Look around you carefully. Try to notice every detail of your surroundings. Now close your eyes and get ready to test your memory! Get your friend to ask you a question such as: "Is there a shark in the a painting on the wall?" or maybe a trickier question such as: "What color is the chair in the corner?" You may keep score and add a point when you get a question right and subtract a point if you miss one. You may take turns asking the questions.

Created and written by Mary Ellen McKee, age 11

- -

ANSWER TO CROSSWORD PUZZLE ON PAGE 18

- -

ANSWER TO WORD SEARCH ON PAGE 35

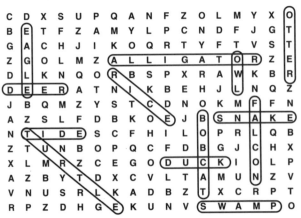

INDEX